Single and Saved:
Waiting for Mr. Right

Single and Saved: Waiting for Mr. Right

Kianna Renay Brooks

Little Rock, Arkansas

J. Kenkade Publishing
6104 Forbing Rd
Little Rock, AR 72209
www.jkenkade.com
Facebook.com/JKenkade

J. Kenkade Publishing is a registered trademark.

Printed in the United States of America
ISBN 978-1-955186-07-0

Single and Saved: Waiting for Mr. Right

Kianna Renay Brooks

Single and Saved: Waiting for Mr. Right

J. Kenkade Publishing
6104 Forbing Rd
Little Rock, AR 72209
www.jkenkade.com
Facebook.com/JKenkade

J. Kenkade Publishing is a registered trademark.

Printed in the United States of America
ISBN 978-1-955186-07-0

Dedication

I dedicate this book to all single Christians around the globe. Single and Saved: Waiting for Mr. Right is a book that was written for Christian men and women to help them find their God-given spouses. This book will teach Christians how to wait on God for their soulmates. I believe that many believers find it hard to wait on God for true love. Throughout the book, the Holy Spirit will teach us how to remain faithful unto Him until they come. Some Christians may struggle with finding "the one". When you read and study this book, God will begin to reveal to you who your spouse may be. After He shows you, pray and ask Him to keep you until they come. Know that all things are possible with God, so He will provide everything that you may lack or need as you wait. Lastly, the vision for this book is to inspire, empower, and enlighten saved singles across the globe as they wait for their Mr. or Mrs. Right!

Table of Contents

Opening Prayer

"Therefore I say unto you, What things soever ye desire, when ye pray, believe that ye receive them, and ye shall have them."
Mark 11:24

Dear Heavenly Father,

I come to you in the name of Jesus, praying for all of those who may come in contact with this book. I asked that it touches the lives of those who are in Christ, whether they are saved Christians or unbelievers. If they are not saved, show them that they cannot live without You. Also, forgive them for their sins. I ask that You give them the spirit of discernment to know that it was You who has written this book and not me. As they begin to read this book, give them spiritual knowledge through studying and reading Your Word. As they study, teach them how to wait on You for their true loves, so You can bless them with their future spouses. Let them know that even though they may desire spouses at this time, they still have to wait on You for their arrivals. As they wait, prepare them to become the husbands or wives that You have called them to be. Even when times may become hard, keep them so they won't fall into the hands of temptation. Bind all distractions that may come and keep their minds focused on You, Lord! While they wait, if the devil tries to bring demonic forces to attack them, keep them and protect them so the demonic forces will flee. Ephesians 6:12 says, "For we wrestle not against flesh and blood, but against principalities, against powers, against the rulers of the darkness of this world, against spiritual wickedness in high places." I claim today that every person who reads this book will receive their God-given spouse. I dispatch angels of the living God to cover them, protect them, and send them their future spouses in Jesus' name. Romans 4:17 says, "...I have made thee a father of many nations,) before Him whom he believed, even God, who quickeneth the dead, and calleth those things which are not as though they were."

Dear God, as we begin to read, guide us with Your truth and allow this book to become a blessing to all of those who may read it.

In Jesus' name, I pray. Amen!

Introduction

Hi there! Are you ready to find the person God has designed for you? Marriage is a beautiful thing. Looking for your soulmate isn't always easy, but reading this book will help you find them. Genesis 2:18 says, "And the Lord God said, It is not good that the man should be alone; I will make him an help meet for him." Genesis 2:22-24 says, "And the rib, which the Lord God had taken from man, made he a woman, and brought her unto the man. And Adam said, This is now bone of my bones, and flesh of my flesh: she shall be called Woman, because she was taken out of Man. Therefore shall a man leave his father and his mother, and shall cleave unto his wife: and they shall be one flesh." Before you can become one flesh with your future spouse, you have to find them first. Matthew 7:7 says, "Ask, and it shall be given you; seek, and ye shall find; knock, and it shall be opened unto you..." If you want to find your true love, you have to ask God who the spouse that He desires for you to have is. As you begin to grow in knowledge, allow God to show you who will become your future spouse. Then, once they arrive, you can start a new journey of sharing true love with them. Take this spiritual knowledge and apply it to your everyday life so that when your spouse comes, you will be prepared to receive them. John 16:13 says, "Howbeit when he, the Spirit of truth, is come, he will guide you into all truth: for he shall not speak of himself; but whatsoever he shall hear, that shall he speak: and he will shew you things to come." In conclusion, read your way into a deeper relationship with God and a healthier relationship with your partner that will lead to a beautiful marriage. Through the leading of the Holy Spirit, you will be able to walk away with a new and refreshed spirit that will help prepare you for marriage. Without further ado, let's get started!

Chapter 1

†

Single and Saved

"And the rib, which the Lord God had taken from man, made he a woman, and brought her unto the man. And Adam said, this is now bone of my bones, and flesh of my flesh: she shall be called Woman, because she was taken out of Man. Therefore shall a man leave his father and his mother, and shall cleave unto his wife: and they shall be one flesh."
Genesis 2:22-24

Living a Single Lifestyle as a Christian

Isaiah 41:10 says, " Fear thou not; for I am with thee: be not dismayed; for I am thy God: I will strengthen thee; yea, I will help thee; yea, I will uphold thee with the right hand of my righteousness."

1 Corinthians 7:8 (ESV) says, "To the unmarried and the widows I say that it is good for them to remain single, as I am."

Live Your Life with a Purpose

Jeremiah 29:11 says, "For I know the thoughts that I think toward you, saith the Lord, thoughts of peace, and not of evil, to give you an expected end."

Commit Yourself to Purity

Matthew 5:8 says, "Blessed are the pure in heart: for they shall see God."

Lead and Draw People to Christ

John 12:32 says, "And I, if I be lifted up from the earth, will draw all men unto me."

Connect with God on a Personal Level

2 Chronicles 7:14 says, "If my people, which are called by my name, shall humble themselves, and pray, and seek my face, and turn from their wicked ways; then will I hear from heaven, and will forgive their sin, and will heal their land."

1 Chronicles 22:19 says, "Now set your heart and your soul to seek the Lord your God; arise therefore, and build ye the sanctuary of the Lord God, to bring the ark of the covenant of the Lord, and the holy vessels of God, into the house that is to be built to the name of the Lord."

Get Connected with Close Friends

John 15:12-15 says, "This is my commandment, That ye love one another, as I have loved you. Greater love hath no man than this, that a man lay down his life for his friends. Ye are my friends, if ye do whatsoever I command you. Henceforth I call you not servants; for the servant knoweth not what his lord doeth: but I have called you friends; for all things that I have heard of my Father I have made known unto you."

Serve the Lord and Others

1 Samuel 12:24 says, "Only fear the Lord, and serve him in truth with all your heart: for consider how great things he hath done for you."

John 12:26 says, "If any man serve me, let him follow me; and where I am, there shall also my servant be: if any man serve me, him will my Father honour."

Stay Focused on Your God-Given Assignment

Philippians 3:15 (MSG) says, "So let's keep focused on that goal, those of us who want everything God has for us. If any of you have something else in mind, something less than total commitment, God will clear your blurred vision– you'll see it yet..."

Matthew 6:33 says, "But seek ye first the kingdom of God, and his righteousness; and all these things shall be added unto you."

"A fairytale only has a happy ending when the Queen waits for her King to arrive. Trust the process; it's worth the wait."
– Kianna Brooks

What classifies you as being "single"? Being single simply means that you have never been married, you have gotten a divorce, or you are a widow or a widower. When you are put in the category of being "single", that means that you no longer look at singleness as an option but rather the way that you have chosen to live your life. Being single is a choice to refuse to let your life be defined by your relationship status and live every day happily, allowing your "ever after" to work itself out. The spiritual definition of "being single" is patiently waiting on the person who God has ordained for you to have. When a man is not looking for a woman, that's when he finds her; when a woman is not looking for a man, that's generally when he comes.

Singleness is a Gift from God

Singleness is the quality or state of being single or being separate from all others. When you are single, you have more time to focus on yourself and others and devote yourself unto the Lord. Sometimes we can take being single for granted, but singleness can give you more time to work on you and your purpose and allow God to purify your heart while you are waiting for your spouse.

Most single people haven't chosen singleness, but there are a few people who have devoted themselves to staying single and doing Christian work. When you are single, you have some advantages that other people don't have, such as freedom, more space, a freer schedule, more alone time, living by yourself, and more time to serve the Lord. Take advantage of being single and use that free time to witness to other people, work with the youths at your local church, help out with the finances, or teach a Bible study class. When you are married, you are restricted from doing a lot of these things because you have to consider how you and your partner will spend your free time. Most of your time may go to holidays, anniversaries, planning vacations, daily menus for the household, and raising your children. An unmarried man is concerned about the Lord's affairs and how he can please the Lord, and a married man is concerned about the affairs of this world and how he can please his wife. Take singleness as a blessing because you can fully devote yourself unto serving God and doing His work.

How Does God View Singles?

I read an article entitled "4 Things God Says to Singles" by Vaughan Robertson. In the article, he states that a person should receive their situation in life, whether single or married, as "a gift of God's grace". Some may ask, "What if I don't think I have the gift of singleness?" or "What if I don't find it easy being on my own and I long to be married?"

"Marriage is good," he stated. "But so is singleness." When Paul speaks of singleness as a gift, he isn't speaking of a particular ability; he's saying that some people have to be contentedly single, which means in a way that expresses happiness or satisfaction. He is also speaking of the state of being single. So, as long as you have it, it's a gift from God, just as marriage will be God's gift to you if you ever receive it.

There are many great blessings in marriage, but there are difficulties also. Christian couples don't often talk openly about the hard things they face in marriage, which can give singles a different view of marriage. We, as singles, can see marriage as such a beautiful thing, but there are some downfalls that come with being married. Even when married couples' relationships are good, sometimes life can be more complicated. That's why, as singles, we shouldn't focus on the difficulties of being single as some do; we should make the most of it by taking advantage of God's gift of singleness while we have it. (I would like to give credit to Vaughan Robertson at thegospelcoalition.org for the information that is provided up above.)

Singleness

I often hear people say, "God's got somebody out there for everybody." Sadly, all godly people will not get married! Elizabeth Woodson once said this: "God knows what's best for His people; many will live their best life without a spouse and biological children. These people will know God more deeply, serve Him more powerfully, and experience greater joy than they could have as married people. This is not because singleness is better but because marriage wasn't a part of God's perfect will for their life."

So, I asked God, "Is this statement true? Is there somebody out there for everybody? Is every Christian fit for marriage?"

God replied with these words: "No, everyone is not designed for marriage. I have set aside those who I've called to be married and those who I have chosen to live a single life and serve Me. Once I have seen that a person has grown spiritually and reached a certain level of maturity and understanding, their faithfulness will show Me that they have reached the capacity where they are comfortable serving Me for the rest of their life, and they will be okay with being single and by themselves. So, that's when I will send them the person who will push them closer to Me and not away from Me. I will never send you someone who will get your focus off of

Me; I will send you someone who will help you grow in Me. The love that you will have for one another will draw you closer together as one. You will keep Christ at the center of your relationship, and you will never love one another more than you love God. As you grow deeper in Christ, I will show your man that he has found his wife. Then he will know that I have destined you for marriage. You will become his helpmate, and you will spend the rest of your lives growing in Christ and serving Me as your Lord and Savior."

Matthew 19:11-12 (MSG) says, "But Jesus said, Not everyone is mature enough to live a married life. It requires a certain aptitude and grace. Marriage isn't for everyone. Some, from birth seemingly, never give marriage a thought. Others never get asked—or accepted. And some decide not to get married for kingdom reasons. But if you're capable of growing into the largeness of marriage, do it."

Every single person has a different experience than another. Some things that may bother one person may not affect someone else who's single. To me, one of the hardest things about being single is being alone. I often hear most single people complain about spending their holiday seasons by themselves. If you look on the calendar, there are six important dates out of the year that we celebrate. Birthdays, Christmas, Thanksgiving, fourth of July, Valentine's Day, and New

Year's. Some people may ask, "What are some different activities that singles can do during the holiday season instead of spending them alone?" The following are some great activities that singles can do during the holiday season.

Activities for Singles during the Holiday Season

Birthdays

1. Set up a lunch date with some of your friends.
2. Throw yourself a nice birthday party.
3. Go to the movies.
4. Plan a spa day and get a full facial makeover.
5. Go get a full-body couple's massage with some of your friends.
6. Buy yourself a gift.

New Year's

1. Light up a candle, open up some sparkling water, and give a toast to yourself.
2. Get dressed up nice.
3. Find a nice, elegant restaurant and go out for the night.
4. Have a New Year's party with some of your family and friends.
5. Go watch a fireworks show.
6. Go to a New Year's service at church.
7. Clean out your closet and start the New Year off fresh.
8. Make a New Year's resolution.

Valentine's Day

1. Invite some people over to your home and host a "singles only" dinner party.

2. Treat yourself to a movie.

3. Go to a nice, elegant restaurant.

4. Buy yourself some candy, a teddy bear, and some white chocolate strawberries.

5. Men, treat yourself to a nice haircut.

6. Ladies, go get your hair and nails done.

7. Plan a Valentine's Day weekend getaway with some of your single friends.

Fourth of July

1. Barbecue.

2. Pop some fireworks.

3. Go to your local shopping mall and hang out with some of your friends.

4. Go bike riding.

5. Go watch a fireworks show.

6. Celebrate on the beach.

7. Have a family gathering at a local park.

8. Go swimming.

9. Watch a parade.

10. Take a vacation.

Thanksgiving

1. Cook a big Thanksgiving dinner and invite some of your friends over to share it with you.

2. Play some card games with your family and friends.

3. Make a Thanksgiving snack bag filled with treats of your choice.

4. Plan a family trip.

5. Watch an NFL football game with your family.

6. Go to a Thanksgiving service at your local church home.

Christmas

1. Sing Christmas carols to the people in your neighborhood.

2. Spend time with your family.

3. Light up some cinnamon candles so that the smell can get you in the Christmas spirit.

4. Go to a Christmas parade.

5. Watch Christmas movies.

6. Wrap up some Christmas gifts and give them out to family members and friends.

7. Buy yourself a nice gift and put it under the tree.

8. Bake some cookies for Santa and leave them under the tree.

9. Play Secret Santa with your friends.

10. Have the gift of giving by doing Christmas giveaways.

11. Acknowledge that it's Jesus' birthday and celebrate it at your local church.

Living a Saved Lifestyle as a Christian

We often hear people say that they are Christians, but their lifestyle doesn't back up what they say. You'll notice the first part of the word "Christian" is "Christ-". So, that means if you are going to live a Christian lifestyle, then the people of the world and the people in the church should see Christ in you before they see you. If you are going to live a godly lifestyle, then your actions should back up the religion that you have chosen if you have chosen to serve the Lord. By faith, we live out what the Word of God says. We should read His Word, walk in truth, and believe His Word because we are saved by the Word of God. Ephesians 2:8-9 says, "For by grace are ye saved through faith; and that not of yourselves: it is the gift of God..."

Being saved is when you have accepted Jesus Christ as your Lord and Savior. What does it mean to accept Jesus Christ as your Lord and Savior? That's when you have received the baptism of the Holy Ghost and allowed Jesus Christ to come into your life and purify your heart by dying to your fleshly desires and doing the will of Jesus Christ. Being saved is not just a walk with Christ; it is a journey through life. You have to be willing to sacrifice your fleshly desires by submitting yourself to the will of God. Giving yourself to God is not just giving Him your life; it is giving Him your soul as well.

I read an article by The People of the United Methodist Church that stated, "Being saved means turning away from a life that is without God, that is focused solely upon ourselves. It means giving up the obsession with our needs, our wants, our pleasures, our comforts, our importance, our egos, and our power and [doing] the will of God!" In the article, the writer also went on to explain, "...being saved in the Christian faith is really a two-part experience: being saved from something and being saved to something. You are being saved from the sins of the world by submitting your life unto the hands of Christ."

God has saved us Christians from partaking in alcohol abuse, drugs, lustful sins, sexual misuse, submitting to a "higher power", serving idol gods, unbelief, abuse, pursuit of money at the expense of others, pride, blaspheming the Holy Spirit, and breaking any of God's commandments. Our lives are changed by God and by us doing the will of God. Living this faith daily is a greater priority than our own will. As Christians, we should know that being saved and serving the people of God are more important than anything else other than our salvation. Romans 10:9-10 instructs us: "That if thou shalt confess with thy mouth the Lord Jesus, and shalt believe in thine heart that God hath raised him from the dead, thou shalt be saved. For with the heart man believeth unto righteousness; and with the mouth confession is made unto salvation."

Date: ____________________

NOTES

____
____
____
____
____
____
____
____
____
____
____
____
____
____
____
____
____
____
____
____
____

"Only fear the Lord, and serve him in truth with all your heart: for consider how great things he hath done for you."
1 Samuel 12:24

Chapter 2

†

Letting Go of Your Past

"Forget the former things;
do not dwell on the past."
Isaiah 43:18 (NIV)

Letting Go of the Dead Weight from Your Past

Revelation 21:4 (ESV) says, "He will wipe away every tear from their eyes, and death shall be no more, neither shall there be mourning, nor crying, nor pain anymore, for the former things have passed away." Sometimes in life, we try to hold on to things that are dead weight to us. People who are dead weight to you will try to make you feel like you cannot live without them. Eventually, you will have to let those people go. If you don't, they will become toxic to you. When a person becomes toxic to you, it's necessary for you to break up with them.

When you break up with someone, it can be a difficult thing to do because you have to make the decision to release that person from your life. By this time, you realize that this person doesn't embrace you, appreciate you, or value you as a person. Once you realize that you no longer want to be in a relationship with them, you have to move forward with your life! No matter how much you may love them, if they cannot appreciate the person that you are trying to become, then you have to let them go.

"Don't hold on to dead things;
they only weigh you down."
– Kianna Brooks

Letting go of someone is coming to the realization that some people are a part of your history and not a part of your destiny. When someone is a part of your history, that means that they are meant to be in the past tense in your life. But when a person is a part of your destiny, that means you are destined to be with them because God has placed them there. Once you let go of your ex-partner, the relationship that you once had with them should become dead to you (example: feelings, emotions, love, and etc.). I call this a "dead relationship."

Dead relationships are past fellowships that you once had with people who are no longer in your life. Most people lose themselves trying to restore a dead relationship because they are trying to restore something that is not fixable. Some people stick around because they feel like the relationship has potential to work. Once a relationship becomes dead, it should stay that way! Why? Because dead relationships are unhealthy for you, and they can affect the person that you're trying to become.

Many of us are still carrying around dead relationships. The reason why is because we haven't let go of our previous partners. How do you know if you have fully let go of your past? Well, begin to reflect and evaluate.

Ask yourself questions such as these:

"How do I know if I have let go of a dead relationship?"

"What signs show that I'm still attached to my ex-partner?"

- Sign #1: You can't seem to find the person that you once were.
- Sign #2: You find yourself comparing your new partner to your ex-partner's mistakes and flaws.
- Sign #3: You become fearful of dating again.

• Sign #4: You reject anyone who could be good for you because you are used to settling for less.

If you can relate to any of the above, then you are still carrying around a dead relationship. Isaiah 46:2-4 (MSG) says, "Dead weight, burdens who can't bear burdens, hauled off to captivity. Listen to me, family of Jacob, everyone that's left of the family of Israel. I've been carrying you on my back from the day you were born, And I'll keep on carrying you when you're old. I'll be there, bearing you when you're old and gray. I've done it and will keep on doing it, carrying you on my back, saving you."

How would you know if you have let go of the dead weight of your past? You will know because the things that once bothered you won't affect you anymore. You will walk away knowing that everything that once was a dead weight to you doesn't have purpose in your life anymore.

Isaiah 43:18 (NIV) says, "Forget the former things; do not dwell on the past." Most people like to move on to a new relationship without being healed from their last one. This upcoming section will teach you how to move past your past relationship and close that chapter of your life!

"You cannot keep repeating the steps of your past. Leave dead relationships alone and move forward with your life."
– Kianna Brooks

The Hardest Part About Letting Go

Why do you think it's so hard to let go of your past? The hardest part about letting go of someone is trying to move on from a relationship with a person who you may still love and care about. You still have to force yourself to move on even if you wanted the relationship to work. Yes, it may be hard to walk away, but if you don't want to remain sad, depressed, or hurt, then you have to allow them to move on with their life.

You may say, "Well, what do I do if I'm still in love with this person? What if I don't want to let them go?"

My question to you is: Do you understand the importance of letting them go?

When I began to ponder these thoughts, the Lord began to speak to me. The Holy Spirit told me, "Letting go is to let go of any asset that is not healthy for you spiritually, mentally, or emotionally." When I thought about His response, it made me think about this– starting over will help you release yourself from that person. Then this question came to mind: "Why don't we release those things that try to attach themselves to us, whether they are relationships, friendships, or fellowships that we once had with people in the past?" After pondering on this question, I began to study more about letting go.

"It's better to be happy being lonely than to be miserable with someone who doesn't care about you or love you."
– Kianna Brooks

While researching, I found a study that stated, "When you are letting go of your past, that person may still hold a place in your heart, but it is better to let whatever it is go and move forward with your life than to let it hold you down and make you feel depressed." It also stated that you have to "learn how to break down the walls between you and that person and let go of the feelings that you once had tied down with them." That's when I realized that when you do let go of someone who has done wrong by you, you have to forgive yourself for the things that you have allowed them to do to damage you mentally and physically. Once you have decided to let that person go, you have to be willing to allow life to carry you to a new deeper place within yourself.

Some may ask, "How do I move forward with my life? How do I stop communicating with someone from my past who doesn't want to let me go?"

Easy.

Shut off all forms of contact with that person and show them that you are not interested in being in a relationship with them anymore. After being hurt, allow God to heal you and restore your soul. The following section will teach you how to get healed before dating again so you don't bring the hurt from your last relationship into your new one. Proverbs 4:25 (ESV) says, "Let your eyes look directly forward, and your gaze be straight before you."

Letting Go of Your Past

Most people unknowingly decide to get into new relationships without letting go of the dead weight of their past. Before you can start courting again, you have to allow God to heal you. In order for you to let go and walk in prosperity, you have to be healed from the things that hurt you. One form of being hurt is being "damaged". Sometimes, when someone is damaged, they don't realize it until later on in the relationship. When a person is damaged, they become dangerous. Because the person is damaged from what hurt them in the past, their injuries tend to affect the ones around them. They start to hurt those they come in contact with.

Some get into new relationships thinking that their partners can fix the bruises and cuts from their last relationship when, in all reality, they can't. This only damages them and the other person. When you are wounded, you start to bleed on people that didn't cut you. Psalm 147:3 (ESV) says, "He heals the brokenhearted and binds up their wounds." When you are damaged, learn how to forgive the person for what they have done to hurt you and move forward with your life. This next session will teach you how to let go of your past so that you can be healed. Jeremiah 17:14 (ESV) says, "Heal me, O Lord, and I shall be healed; save me, and I shall be saved, for you are my praise."

What wound is affecting your life? What causes you to withdraw from people before they hurt you? A lot of us push our partners away because we are afraid of getting hurt. We are cautious about opening our personal space up to them. We will only share with them what makes us feel comfortable and things that we can protect. Also, some people are more vulnerable than others. Being vulnerable causes people to put their guards up. A lot of people get taken advantage of when they are vulnerable because their partners may feel that they are too weak to stand up for themselves. That's why most people take precautions when they start new relationships. Proverbs 3:29 (MSG) says, "Don't figure ways of taking advantage of your neighbor when he's sitting there trusting and unsuspecting."

Before you start dating again, make sure you are completely healed from your past relationships. How would you know if your last relationship has left you hurt or broken? You would still dwell on the past by always bringing up past events in your life or you would constantly find yourself complaining about the things that your ex has done to hurt you. If you are doing this, then you are not ready to be dating. Find some alone time with God and get set free!

"You will never get healed from the things of your past if you don't let go."
- Kianna Brooks

If you want to be healed, you have to recognize what hurt you. Jesus died for our sins, and He was bruised for our iniquities. So, if God was able to heal Jesus from the hurt of the world, why do you think He can't heal us from the hurt of the flesh? Isaiah 53:5 says, "But he was wounded for our transgressions, he was bruised for our iniquities: the chastisement of our peace was upon him; and with his stripes we are healed." If you find yourself in such an unpleasant place in your life, learn how to disassociate yourself from those things and that person. Pray and ask God to remove those people from your life. Hebrews 12:1 says, "Wherefore seeing we also are compassed about with so great a cloud of witnesses, let us lay aside every weight, and the sin which doth so easily beset us, and let us run with patience the race that is set before us..."

Rules for Moving Past Your Past Relationship

Rule 5: *Stop allowing them to come by to visit you from time to time.*

If you haven't noticed, sometimes hanging around your ex can stir up some old feelings that you had for them. Just because the relationship is dead, it doesn't mean that you've forgotten about the feelings that you once shared. If you show signs that you still love them, you still have feelings for them, you look lost without them, or show any signs that you are still interested in being with them, then that gives them the indication that you are still available for them. If you keep that door open for too long, then that gives them access back into your life. Your destiny is never tied to those who left, so let them walk! I heard a pastor once say, "If people can walk away from you, let them walk!"

Rule 4: *Go unfriend them on all of your social media accounts.*

Sometimes, seeing your ex being in a happier relationship without you can hurt you. The devil will try to make you feel as if they are living a better life without you in it. When I was dealing with a bad breakup, the enemy would always tell me to go look on my ex's Facebook page to see how they were doing in life. I didn't know that seeing them living well and being happy with someone else was actually hurting me. I continued to complain to the Lord about what they were doing and how bad they played me in the end. The Lord spoke these words to me: "It won't bother you if you can't see it." That's when I had to make the decision to unfriend them, block them, and move on with my life!

Rule 3: When someone from your past texts you out of the blue, don't reply back to their text message.

Some people do that to see how far you will let them go. Others try to see if they are able to come back into your life. I had to learn that when you are trying to let go of someone, you can't continue to communicate with them because not everything needs closure or requires a response. My pastor always says this: "When nothing is said, a response is not required!"

Rule 2: Stop picking up the phone to talk to them.

If you're not strong enough to forward their calls, hang up in their face or delete their number out of your phone. Then, allow the phone to do it for you and block them.

Rule 1: *If your ex-partner keeps calling you and you don't want to talk to them, then do not respond to them.*

As long as you respond to people who are not a necessity to you, then you give them leeway to continue to bother you.

Date: ___________________

NOTES

____

____

____

____

____

____

____

____

____

____

____

____

____

____

____

____

____

____

____

____

____

"But I say unto you, Love your enemies, bless them that curse you, do good to them that hate you, and pray for them which despitefully use you, and persecute you..."

Matthew 5:44

Chapter 3

†

Know Your Worth

"Who can find a virtuous woman?
For her price is far above rubies."
Proverbs 31:10

Understanding Your Value

1. Do you know your worth?

YES OR **NO**

2. Do you battle with low self-esteem?

YES OR **NO**

3. Do you feel like you're good enough or pretty enough?

YES OR **NO**

4. Is this statement true for you? "There are many things that I don't like about myself."

YES OR **NO**

Explain below:

____

____

____

____

____

5. Do you say more positive things or negative things about yourself?

____

____

____

____

____

6. Why is having self-confidence so important? And do you have confidence in yourself?

____

____

____

____

____

7. Do you feel that other people may think poorly of you and your appearance?

YES OR **NO**

Explain below:

____

____

____

____

____

8. When you are reflecting about your personal appearance, what is your main focus? Do you focus more on what you have to offer as a person or what you are missing as a person?

____

____

____

____

____

Understanding Your Value & Knowing Your Worth

Earlier, we answered questions about understanding our value and knowing our worth. While focusing on this topic, we were able to discuss how we view ourselves as individuals. When you think about the definition of "value", you have to understand that it is the worth of a person and how they may carry themselves as a human being. Another form of feeling worthless is having low self-esteem. When a person struggles with low self-esteem, they begin to settle for something below their worth. They complain about their personal appearance and reject the person that God sees.

During my study of this topic, the Holy Spirit began to tell me that a lot of people battle with low self-esteem because they don't know their value as individuals or how much they are worth to Him. That's when I realized that if a person does not know their own worth as a human being, then they will never understand how valuable they are to God and someone else. I read a quote once: "Don't let anyone that doesn't know your value determine your worth." To be able to determine your worth, you have to pray and ask the Holy Spirit to show you how valuable you are to Him!

Next, if you begin to read the Word of God, He will begin to show you that you cannot find your value or worth in man, but you can find it in Him. Jeremiah 17:7 (NIV) says, "But blessed is the one who trusts in the Lord, whose confidence is in him." Now that you know that your confidence is found in God, don't settle below your worth, but continue to strive towards becoming the person who God has created you to be. If you stay humble unto God, He will begin to teach you how to carry yourself until your spouse arrives. As you begin to understand your worth, make sure that you only date those who see you the way that God sees you. Pray that they understand your value and accept you for your worth. Pray that this person will be loyal, faithful, trustworthy, and love God more than they love themselves. While you are waiting, ask God to help you find a spouse with these characteristics. Know that the key to finding them is remaining patient and waiting until God sends them to you. Make sure that you carry yourself with a high standard to where they know that they have to be worthy enough to have you. In this next session, the Holy Spirit will teach us our worth and how to walk in it with confidence while we wait for our soulmate. As you begin to learn these empowerments, begin to speak them over your life daily so that you can build up your confidence in Christ!

LOOK AT YOUR REFLECTION IN A MIRROR.

Job 33:4 says, "The spirit of God hath made me, and the breath of the Almighty hath given me life." You are created by the world's greatest artist (which is God), so when you take that first step to look in the mirror, stop and observe yourself and look at the beautiful creation that God has made. Sometimes, the devil can try to make us feel like we were an accident and God made a mistake when He created us. Well, I'm here to let you know that you were designed for a purpose. So, when God created you, He didn't make any mistakes. Genesis 1:31 says, "And God saw everything that he had made, and, behold, it was very good..." So, no matter what the enemy tries to say, denounce it and know that you were created beautifully in the image of Jesus Christ.

EMBRACE YOUR BEAUTY.

Embrace the person who God has called you to be and fall in love with that person. Learn how to love yourself inside and out and always remember that you are one of God's beautiful creations. He made a masterpiece when He designed you! Ephesians 2:10 says, "For we are his workmanship, created in Christ Jesus unto good works, which God hath before ordained that we should walk in them." Begin to embrace who you are in God because Psalm 139:14 says, "I will praise thee;

for I am fearfully and wonderfully made: marvellous are thy works; and that my soul knoweth right well." Speak this scripture over your life daily, and while you're saying it, allow God to show you how to embrace who you are in Him!

DEVELOP SELF-LOVE.

Love is an intense feeling of deep affection for someone, so before a man or woman can love you to the fullest, you have to learn how to love yourself first. Allow the word "love" to become an action and not just a feeling. Self-love is being happy with your own well-being and having true happiness. Show yourself love by giving yourself the things that you desire without sinning against the Word of God. Always remember that self-love is the best love. 1 John 4:16 (NIV) says, "And so we know and rely on the love God has for us. God is love. Whoever lives in love lives in God, and God in them."

SET A STANDARD FOR YOURSELF.

Set a standard for yourself that will build you up for success! People who set a standard for themselves walk with class, expect the finer things in life, go after their dreams and vision, and walk like they already have them. You can do the same thing! Set a standard that is best for you. Pray over that standard and ask God if that is the best route for you to take. Once He gives you an answer, start to live by this standard and don't allow anyone to make you lose your focus. Romans 12:2 (GNT) says, "Do not conform yourselves to the standards of this world, but let God transform you inwardly by a complete change of your mind. Then you will be able to know the will of God – what is good and is pleasing to him and is perfect." Always follow your heart, and He with you every step of the way!

WALK WITH CONFIDENCE.

Walking with confidence is not being prideful, arrogant, or acting high-minded; rather, it means that you carry yourself with high standards. Having confidence is knowing your value as a person, understanding your personality traits, keeping a positive mindset about yourself, and visualizing yourself as what you want to be. Know that having confidence is not just about being beautiful; it is how you carry yourself as a person. As long as you remember this, then you will never change your character and you will always remain humble. 1 John 2:6 says, "He that saith he abideth in him ought himself also so to walk, even as he walked." Build up your confidence and self-esteem by walking in the same footsteps of Jesus Christ. Walking in His footsteps simply means that you will follow behind Him and walk in the path that He has created for you. Jeremiah 29:11 says, "'For I know the thoughts I think toward you, saith the Lord, thoughts of peace, and not of evil, to give you an expected end.'" Therefore, you are the child of a king, so learn how to walk with your head held high and never down low. Continue to build your confidence in God, and He will build His confidence in you! Isaiah 32:17 (NIV) says, "The fruit of that righteousness will be peace; its effect will be quietness and confidence forever."

Date: ____________________

NOTES

____

____

____

____

____

____

____

____

____

____

____

____

____

____

____

____

____

____

____

____

____

"For we are his workmanship, created in Christ Jesus unto good works, which God hath before ordained that we should walk in them."

Ephesians 2:10

Chapter 4

†

The Difference Betweeen A Church Man and A Godly Man

"And Jacob served seven years to get Rachel; and they seemed unto him but a few days, For the love he had to her."
Genesis 29:20

A Church Man Vs. A Godly Man

For the sake of this chapter, I will express my preference between church men and godly men. Through studying and praying, I have found out that there's a difference between the two. Throughout this chapter, I will refer to modern-day church-going men as "church men" and true, authentic, God-fearing men as "godly men". The definitions that will be given to you down below will help you understand the difference between the two. This section is not to bash any man that goes to church, but it is to help "godly women" decipher the true from the false.

Some men are conformed to the world and not by the Spirit of God. When a man is conformed to the world, he's going to do it the world's way and not God's way. I refer to those men as "church men". Modern-day church-going men try to do things that are pleasing to the world. Unknowingly, their hearts' desires are not after God. Alternatively, "godly men" are men who seek after God's heart. A godly man's heart desires what God desires. In other words, a "godly man" is conformed to the Spirit of God and not to the world.

When it comes to waiting for a godly man, how can we discern the true from the false? How do we know the difference between church men and godly men? When I began to think on these questions, the Holy Spirit began to reveal to me His perspective on this topic. So that you can understand the difference between the two, I would like to focus on these questions by sharing with you God's response to me. In this next session, God will teach us how to discern a church man from a godly man.

A Church Man

What is a church man? Church-going men are men who go to church faithfully every Sunday. They feel that going to church week after week will validate them to still live a sinful lifestyle. These men are not saved because they are not true men of God. They are faithless, they never move by the Spirit of God, they are always led by their flesh, and they think that serving the Lord in attendance will be pleasing unto God. God spoke to my spirit and said, "Just because a man has a perfect attendance record at church, it doesn't make him godly!" He also said, "Your attendance at church isn't the only thing that pleases Me. It is your faithfulness unto Christ and your daily walk with Me that captures My attention."

When you are a single Christian woman waiting for a godly man, how do you know if they are godly or ungodly? A "church man" and a "ungodly man" are recognized as the same thing, so how will you know the real from the fake? Well, this next part will teach you about the four types of ungodly men. We discussed earlier how the first one is not saved, because he is conformed to the world. The second type of ungodly man is referred to as a "benchwarmer" because he never pays attention to the Word of God when it is being brought forth. As for the third and fourth kinds of ungodly men, one upholds a title within the church and the other one dresses to impress the congregation. If you are a Christian woman who is waiting on God for her spouse, don't allow the devil to deceive you into thinking that these men are saved men because they're not. If you are a woman who has been approached by one of the men listed above, then he is not the one. The best thing for you to do is continue to wait for God to send you your spouse.

The Different Types of Ungodly Men

Another form of a church-going man is being a "benchwarmer". A benchwarmer is a man who goes to church just to say he has gone to church on Sunday. These men never allow their spirits to get fed by the Word of God. These men never pay attention when the Word is being brought forth. During service, their attention is captured by something that is not important at the time such as being on their phones, making jokes, playing around, or being flirtatious with some of the sisters in the church. These are distractions that normally take their focus off of the Word of God.

If they are playing in service, how can they be conformed to the Word? That's when you have to ask yourself, "Are they living by the Word of God? Are they really allowing the Holy Spirit to come in and change their life through the message?" The answer is no! You can't play the whole church service and say you got something out of the Word. One thing has their attention more than the other thing does. If you go to church on Sunday and so happen to run across a person who just rides the bench week after week, then move! Because the devil can use anything they do as a distraction to you to get your focus off the Word of God.

Next, some ungodly "church men" hold positions at their churches. Even though they may participate in ministry faithfully, it doesn't make them godly men. Most ungodly men who hold positions in the church begin to misuse their title. Some use it to have authority over others because they like being in control while others use it to get women, to have power, to gain money, or to have sexual relationships with people within the congregation. Because people will see them active in ministry, this can make them ignore the fact that they are playing church. Their lack of knowledge will cause many people in that congregation to fail. Why? Because the enemy has crept in. The Lord would have to come in and show His people that these are not real men of God. Once He does so, they will have to repent and ask God for forgiveness so that they can be delivered.

Also, most women are attracted to men who have big titles in the church. They think that this makes the men more anointed than the other men within the church. Some women feel that men with big titles are special because they're not on the same level as the other members at the church. Some of these women try to become flirtatious with these men, not knowing that this can become a distraction to the men if they're not strong-minded. If the men realize that they have gained attention from these women, then it can become a problem. Their lustful eyes can make them weak to their flesh and will cause them to dishonor God through sinning. If a man is not strong enough, then this will cause him to fall. Godly women have to understand that a true man of God won't fall into the hands of temptation. He will flee from it. Remember, ladies – their position in the church doesn't classify them as godly men, but their titles just hold them to higher responsibilities than the other men in the congregation.

"A title doesn't certify them; God does."
– Kianna Brooks

The last type of ungodly man that we'll discuss will be the one who "dresses up" for church every Sunday. He thinks that wearing a nice suit to service makes him a godly man when it doesn't. He wears name-brand items to make sure they are noticed by people. This man is prideful and arrogant, and he likes to be seen. He feels like his clothes have to make a statement. He treats church as a fashion show. I want you to know that there is nothing wrong with dressing up for church, but if you are more excited about what you are wearing to church on Sunday than hearing the Word of God, then you need to take a step back and review yourself. Know that God doesn't look at the outward apparel– He looks at the heart. Your clothes mean nothing if your heart is not right with God!

A Godly Man

In the previous section, we talked about ungodly men and how their ways are not God's ways. In this section, let's focus on the characteristics of a "godly man". Jesus is the perfect example of how to become a godly man. He demonstrates in His Word how to become more like Him. Christian men should strive to become more like God. Once you make that your main focus, then He will build you into the man that He wants you to be. When I began to study scriptures about godly men, this particular scripture in Psalms captured my attention. Psalm 37:23 says, "The steps of a good man are ordered by the Lord: and he delighteth in his way." This scripture teaches godly men how to allow God to order their footsteps so that God can direct their path in the way that they should go. Allowing God to order your footsteps means to walk with Jesus Christ and to allow Him to build you up in Him and His Word. Unfortunately, all men don't allow the Lord to order their footsteps. Some go based off of how they feel and what their flesh tells them to do. Men who operate by their flesh are not being true men of God. Ladies, you don't want to date men who are moved by their flesh; you want men who will move by the Holy Spirit of God. A godly man will always be led by the Spirit of God, and he will continue to be faithful unto God and ministry. If you wait for a godly man, then God will lead him to you.

Knowing the Characteristics of a Godly Man

Genesis 1:27 says, "So God created man in his own image, in the image of God created he him; male and female created he them." How do you know if he is a true man of God? Easy. Look at his character. God tells us in His Word that we were created in His image. A godly man is going to try his best to display the image of God. He will make sure his life stays holy unto Him. Therefore, he will save himself through purity while he waits for his wife.

Besides waiting for his wife, a godly man knows that having Jesus Christ as his Lord and Savior is the best gift that he can receive. Because he loves God, he will make it his duty to serve God with all of his heart. The Lord told me, "A godly man's focus is on serving Me and pleasing Me. His desire is to serve Me with all of his heart while he focuses on reaching his destiny." Then He said, "Wait for a man that will serve Me because if you wait on a man that will serve Me, then he will serve you as a husband."

"A man who will serve God will serve you."
– Kianna Brooks

In conclusion, throughout this chapter we learned that church men operate under false pretenses and in a way that isn't real while godly men try to have the identity of Christ by showing godly character. Ladies, start observing the men you are dating and make sure that they have the characteristics of godly men. The way that you will know that a man is a godly man is easy. He will pray for you, love you like Jesus loves the church, and help build you to become a better woman each day. If he is God-sent, you won't find him – he will find you. Godly women, pray and ask God to give you the patience to wait on the person that He has for your life! Proverbs 18:22 says, "Whoso findeth a wife findeth a good thing, and obtaineth favour of the Lord."

The Characteristics of a Godly Man

- He strives to become a better man each day.
- He's truthful.
- He's prayerful.

- He remains sacred unto God.
- He asks God to teach him how to be more like Christ.
- He tries to live the life that Christ lived.
- He will receive the Holy Spirit of God. (1 Corinthians 14:2)
- He will serve God and the church.
- He will follow behind Christ, and he puts on the mind of Christ.
- He tries to remain humble as he grows in Christ.
- He will try his best to follow the Word of God.
- He will align his life to the Bible.
- He knows the Word speaks truth. So, if he sees something that is not aligned with God's Word, then he will try to correct it.
- He will use his life as a light to get others saved.
- During service, you will find a godly man praising God and worshipping Him.
- He cares about the concerns of others.
- He will remain in purity.
- He will not be in a rush to get married; he will wait for God to send him his wife.
- He will love a woman like Christ loves the church.
- He will build his relationship off a godly foundation.

Date: ____________________

NOTES

____
____
____
____
____
____
____
____
____
____
____
____
____
____
____
____
____
____
____
____
____
____

"The steps of a good man are ordered by the Lord: and he delighteth in his way." Psalm 37:23

Chapter 5

†

The Process of Waiting-
Patience is the Key

"Wait on the Lord: be of good courage, and he shall strengthen thine heart: wait, I say, on the Lord." Psalm 27:14

Waiting for Your Mr. or Mrs. Right

Life is an ongoing journey, and everyone who desires to get married has to go through the process of waiting for their spouse. While I was studying the Word of God, He showed me that the key to waiting for your spouse is having patience and being faithful unto Him until they come. Being patient is accepting or tolerating a delay without getting angry or upset. When you are waiting for your spouse to come, it requires you to wait on God's timing. Sometimes, waiting on your spouse to arrive can make you feel like there's a delay in God's timing and they will never show up. When we feel like this, God has to constantly remind us that having patience is the key to receiving them. God shared this with me: "When you are being patient and waiting for your spouse to come, don't focus on the delay of the time that it takes for them to get here, but use this time during the delay to prepare yourself for them until they arrive!" Therefore, you should know that all delays are not always bad for you, but if you find yourself in one, then ask God what you should work on during this free time while you are waiting for your spouse to come. Next, the following section will teach you the importance of waiting and how to have patience while you are waiting for your spouse.

"Patience is the key to waiting;
trust the process."
– Kianna Brooks

Having patience requires you to wait, and sometimes it's hard to remain humble until God sends your spouse. Waiting for them to come into your life may make you feel like you have to stay or remain in one particular place for a long period of time. As you wait for your soulmate, God will begin to teach you step by step the process of waiting and how to wait for them. While waiting, use this time wisely by allowing God to teach you. Know that He will put you in a position where you are preparing yourself for your spouse and marriage. This will be a preparation stage, where girls are being transformed into women and boys will be transformed into men. This time will teach women how to become good wives and show men how to become great husbands.

While God is teaching you, ask Him to transform you into the great spouse He knows that you can be. As you move forward with the process, you have to have patience, stay focused, and be progressive in what God is teaching you. If you want to see yourself progress in these things, then you have to remain humble and be willing to learn from God. No matter how long the processing stage may take, know that every good thing is worth the wait! Psalm 39:7 (MSG) says, "What am I doing in the meantime, Lord? Hoping, that's what I'm doing—hoping."

The Purpose for Waiting

Some people can spot attractive people and automatically think that they have found the one. For others, they are ready to walk down the aisle immediately. Understand that you are not destined to marry every person you meet. Why? Because some of us are trying to marry seasonal people! While waiting, know that God isn't in a rush to bless you with your spouse. Even though you may desire to be married at this appointed time, it doesn't mean that it is your season to be married. Ecclesiastes 3:1 says, "To every thing there is a season, and a time to every purpose under the heaven..." The purpose for waiting for your "Mr. or Mrs. Right" is so you can receive the spouse that God wants you to have. When you are waiting, know that it requires you to put all your trust in God. Proverbs 3:5-6 (ESV) says, "Trust in the Lord with all your heart, and do not lean on your own understanding. In all your ways acknowledge him, and he will make straight your paths." As you wait for your spouse, wait on God to release them into your life. Know that eventually He will place someone in your life who will cherish you and love you just like He does. The way to know that you received a spouse from God will be because they will have the character of Christ. Until then, while God is preparing you for your soulmate, continue to grow in Him. Believe that God will keep His promise to you and one day you will receive the person that He has designed just for you. Luke 1:45 (CEV) says, "The Lord has blessed you because you believed that he will keep his promise."

The Importance of Waiting on God for Your Spouse

As believers in Christ, we have to understand that the reason why it is so important to wait on God for our future spouses is because He has created a person specifically for us. But what if you get tired of waiting and you rush and marry the wrong person? What happens next? Many people become frustrated with their partners because they have chosen the wrong ones. I've learned that when you have married the wrong person, you miss out on the spouse that God had for your life. When some people find out they married the wrong person, they try to get a divorce. The Bible speaks strongly about not getting a divorce. 1 Corinthians 7:10-15 says, "And unto the married I command, yet not I, but the Lord, Let not the wife depart (divorce) from her husband: But and if she depart (divorce), let her remain unmarried or be reconciled to her husband: and let not the husband put away his wife."

Therefore, when you marry the wrong one, you will have to learn how to live with the mistake that you have made. If you would have waited on God, then the spouse that He would have given to you would have been qualified to have you. That's why God requires us to wait on Him. Yes, it may be challenging to wait on God for true love, but the purpose for waiting on God is so that we can receive the person that He desires for us to have. Psalm 27:14 says, "Wait on the Lord: be of good courage, and he shall strengthen thine heart: wait, I say, on the Lord." When it comes to waiting for your spouse, be anxious for nothing, but continue to wait on God and trust His timing! Philippians 4:6 (ESV) says, "Do not be anxious about anything, but in everything by prayer and supplication with thanksgiving let your requests be made known to God."

It's Worth the Wait

Genesis 29:20-21 (ESV) says, "So Jacob served seven years for Rachel, and they seemed to him but a few days because of the love he had for her. Then Jacob said to Laban, 'Give me my wife that I may go in to her, for my time is completed.'" Our gift that comes from waiting is receiving the person that God has destined us to be with. So, let's ask ourselves this question: "Who is worth my time? Is the person that I am waiting for God to send worth it? Am I willing to make a sacrifice just to have them? Do I feel that this person is so valuable to me that I am willing to give up everything just for them?" Well, if you don't know a good explanation for waiting or how to wait, let's read a paraphrased bible story about a man named Jacob. Jacob worked a total of fourteen years for his beloved wife Rachel. This story will teach you about patience, sacrifice, and how to wait on the spouse that God has for you.

In the Old Testament, there is a story about a man by the name of Jacob. He was on a journey, waiting to receive what God had promised him. During his journey, Jacob approached his Uncle Laban's home and fell in love with his cousin Rachel. She became one of the two wives of Jacob. Rachel was Laban's youngest daughter, and Leah was the oldest. Although Jacob wanted Rachel's hand in marriage, he was forced to serve Laban for seven years to have her. Jacob was deceived at the end of that time to marry her sister Leah. Furthermore, Jacob had returned for an additional seven years of labor to be able to win Rachel. Once those seven years were up, then he was allowed to marry Rachel (References: Genesis 29:1-35 ESV, https://www.britannica.com/biography/Rachel-biblical-figure).

Do you believe that Rachel was worth the wait? Would you have been willing to sacrifice fourteen years of your life for the one that you may love? Jacob went through fourteen years of labor for Rachel and showed Laban that he was worthy enough to have her. He not only showed his love for her by waiting but also by sacrificing his time through labor. So, is the person that you are desiring to marry worth waiting for? Will they become the gift that you will receive for waiting?

Because Rachel was Jacob's gift that came from waiting. Once he finally got her, the writer said, "They seemed to him but a few days because of the love he had for her." If you are truly waiting for a God-given spouse, then allow God to send you a spouse like Jacob who doesn't mind serving Him until he finds you!

"There is a person that is out there
waiting for you, but putting your trust
in God and waiting for Him to send them
is the key to finding them."
– Kianna Brooks

Prayer: Waiting for My God-Given Spouse

Lamentations 3:25 says, "The Lord is good unto them that wait for him, to the soul that seeketh him."

Dear Heavenly Father,

I come to you in the name of Jesus, repenting for all of my sins. I do understand that You are the only person that I cannot live without, so I give my life unto You, Lord. Lord, keep me in Your perfect peace as I wait on You for my spouse. Help me to wait on Your timing and not rush the process that You are taking me through. Help me to remain holy without a spot, wrinkle, or blemish just as You desire the church to be when You come back. Ephesians 5:27 (ESV) says, "So that he might present the church to himself in splendor, without spot or wrinkle or any such thing, that she might be holy and without blemish." While I am waiting for my spouse to arrive, give me patience and show me who the one that You have for me is. As I wait, put me in a position where I am preparing myself for them until they come. Until then, don't let me be anxious for anything, but give me understanding to know that everything has an appointed time to come into my life. Lord, You are the example of what I should wait for; make my spouse more like You. In Jesus' name I pray. Amen!

Date: ____________________

NOTES

____
____
____
____
____
____
____
____
____
____
____
____
____
____
____
____
____
____
____
____
____
____

"But if we hope for that we see not,
then do we with patience wait for it."
Romans 8:25

Chapter 6

†

The Process of Dating

"But they that wait upon the Lord shall renew their strength; they shall mount up with wings as eagles; they shall run, and not be weary; and they shall walk, and not faint."
Isaiah 40:31

Part 1: Waiting on God's Perfect Timing

God has a set timing for everything! When you begin to study more about waiting, God will begin to teach you how to wait for a God-given relationship. The reason why He requires us to wait on Him is because He wants us to have a relationship that will be built on the foundation of Christ. Pertaining to marriage, God told us in Genesis 2:18 (ESV), "Then the Lord

God said, 'It is not good that the man should be alone; I will make him a helper fit for him.'" When it comes to marriage, a helpmate is your future spouse. They will be the ones that God will send to help you grow in Him. When you hear scriptures such as these, then it makes you wonder who your helpmate will be. Well, let's see!

Most Christians begin to question God and ask Him, "Will I ever get married? When will this day happen? And where will this moment take place?" Others may wonder, "Where will life take us after we say 'I do'?" Some of us even put God on a deadline and say, "God, if I don't have a spouse by this age, then I'm done looking for love!" Well, think about Ruth in the Bible. Didn't she have to wait for God to send her her Boaz? Didn't Jacob have to work fourteen years just to be able to have Rachel? Everything having to do with your spouse requires you to wait for them. Why? Because your spouse will be assigned to your life from God. No matter how long it takes for them to get here, you are still required to wait for them.

Eventually, God will send this person into your life. Once He does, allow Him to teach you about courting as a believer in Christ. If you are a Christian and you're looking for love, this next part will take you back to the basics and teach you how to date as a Christian.

Courtship & Dating

If you ever decide to date someone, getting to know them is a process. Normally, "dating" is where two people who are attracted to each other spend time together to see if they like each other's company. It may be as short as a week or two, it may take a couple of months, or maybe even years. It all depends on the person. If this is successful, most of the time, they will start to develop a relationship. Courtship is the period of development toward a relationship wherein a couple gets to know each other and decide if there will be an engagement, followed by a marriage. Courtship and dating are not the same thing for Christians as for those who date in the world. Those who are of the world will date by the rules that are given to them by the world or by their fleshly desires whereas those who are Christians will date by the instructions that are given to them by the Holy Spirit who learn how to date through reading the Word of God. I read an article that stated: "Relationships of the world are not built on godly conduct, the Word of God, self-control, or trust, so with these attributes being missing, these types of relationships will fail." Any relationships that are not built on God will fail because they're not built on the foundation of Christ. If your relationship was ordained by God, then it is built to prosper. Romans 12:1-2 (ESV) says, "I appeal to you therefore, brothers, by the mercies of God, to present your bodies as a living sacrifice, holy and acceptable to God, which is your spiritual worship. Do not be conformed to this world, but be transformed by the renewal of your mind, that by testing you may discern what is the will of God, what is good and acceptable and perfect."

The Process of Dating

Developing a relationship with your partner will help you grow a stronger bond. This process will teach you more about them and their personality. While you are getting to know this person, it's okay to go on dates with them. Once you start dating, it will give you a chance to get to know them a little better. When you go on dates, ask them questions like, "What are your goals in life?" or "Do you want to get married in the future?" If you are planning on building a relationship with them, then you should know what their plans are if you decide to get married to them.

Once they share their plans with you, see if they are ambitious about chasing their goals and dreams just like you are. When you are dating, it is important to know if they want to follow their dreams or not. This will tell you more about this person and their mindset. Eventually, once you begin to work on goals with them, their actions will show you if they are really serious about being successful in life.

Next, before you marry this person, make sure they are godly and have the character of Christ. Why? Because if their character is not right with God, then their character will not be right with you.

"Your character should project the image of God and show the love of Christ."
– Kianna Brooks

If you don't see them trying to imitate the identity of Christ, then break up with them. Eventually, this flaw will cause problems in the relationship that will cause it to fail. Therefore, once you start dating, pray and ask God to give you the spirit of discernment so He can show you the things that the enemy might not want you to see. Sometimes, Satan can try to make you ignore the things that God is trying to show you. But if you have the spirit of discernment, then he won't be able to deceive you.

Lastly, while you are courting, don't have sex with your partner before you get to know them because this ruins the process. Most men lose interest in women once they give their bodies to them in the first couple of months. By doing this, there's nothing left for them to wait for. If you give your body to a man before he marries you, then he has no reason to stay with you. You have to make this moment special by waiting. He will respect you and your body more if you wait until the wedding night.

If you want to remain in purity while courting, then follow these few simple steps.

• Step #1: During the process of dating, ask God to teach you how to walk in purity.

• Step #2: You and your partner need to rededicate your bodies unto God.

• Step #3: Read scriptures about purity and saving yourself for marriage.

• Step #4: Learn how to avoid sexual conversations and things that lead to sex.

• Step #5: If you are spending time with your partner and a moment comes that causes you to experience sexual arousal, then leave. Don't allow the devil to put you or your partner in a predicament that will cause you to fall into the hands of temptation. James 4:7 says, "Submit yourselves therefore to God. Resist the devil, and he will flee from you."

Part 2: Building a God-Given Relationship Off the Foundation of Christ

• Allow God to show you who to date.

• Once you start dating, use God as your foundation to start off your relationship.

• Build your relationship on the Word of God.

• Make sure that they are a Christian before you date them, so you won't be unequally yoked. 2 Corinthians 6:14 says, "Be ye not unequally yoked together with unbelievers: for what fellowship hath righteousness with unrighteousness? And what communion hath light with darkness?"

• Before you marry them, seek God's face to make sure that this is the spouse that He desires for you to have.

• Get to know your partner before marriage and learn their likes and dislikes.

• Make goals together as a couple that will be beneficial to your relationship and help prepare you for marriage.

• Once you know that this is the person God has called you to be with for such a time as this, go out and seek godly counsel from a spiritual leader who will lead you back to Christ and help train you on how to date so that once you get married, you can become a better spouse for your partner.

• Take marriage counseling and classes to make sure that this is what you want to do and this is the person who you want to be married to.

• Remain in purity.

• Stay celibate.

• The devil will try to tempt everyone who is in godly relationships, but it is up to us to give that temptation up to God so He can make a way of escape for us because it is He that can keep us from falling.

- Fast and pray for guidance for your relationship so God can continue to do His will for you and your partner's life.
- Once you grow a relationship with God, He will teach you how to grow a relationship with your partner.
- Remain faithful unto God, and He will teach you how to remain faithful to your partner once you get married.

Part 3

LESSON:

Once a month, my pastor leads a marriage workshop to the singles and the married couples at my local church. One night during the marriage workshop, they gave us an activity that we had to fill out with our partner. This activity had materialistic things that could be used to complement our partner's characteristics in the relationship such as being the planner, the organizer, the newspaper, or the one who loves being on time, etc. We had to describe how these terms could apply to us or our relationship. If our partners made us feel like any of the things on this list, then this activity required us to fill in the blanks and write them down. Once we began to realize that these things could relate to us or our partners, then we had to discuss it with the class. Instead of including the whole activity inside of the book, I decided to include the results from this activity. My goal for this lesson is to help couples discuss private conflicts that they may face within their relationships so they can overcome them and move forward with their partner.

ACTIVITY: Particular Roles that are Played in a Relationship

I would like for you to review this lesson with your partner to see in which areas of your relationship you could improve. This activity will show the strengths and weaknesses within the relationship. Once you realize the areas that you or your partner may struggle in, then begin to work on these areas together. Once you finish, read these results with your partner to see which characteristics fit you or them. After reviewing this lesson with them, use this section as an asset to help you guys learn from your previous mistakes. On the following page, use the score sheet to keep tabs on you and your partner's score. Once you go over the activity, put a tally mark down for each area that you thought you or your partner was progressing in or failing in. At the end of the activity, add up the tally marks to see who was the least successful in the relationship. The point of this exercise is not to judge one another; it is to help you improve in the weakest areas of your relationship so you guys can grow together in Christ.

Role: ***Time Management***

- You are the organized person in the relationship; you keep everything on a timely schedule.
- You manage everything in the relationship.
- Being on time is important to you.
- You don't like to be late.
- There's a conflict in the relationship when your partner doesn't go by your set schedule.

Example: John and Sarah are in a relationship. Sarah is good at time management, but sometimes John runs behind schedule. This is a typical problem that they deal with in their relationship. In total, there are five statements on this list that describe their time management skills. Three of these examples describe Sarah, and two of these examples describe John. On the score sheet, Sarah will put down two tally marks by John's name and three by hers. Each tally mark represents what areas they may be strong in or weak in. On the following page, you will find a section called

"Total Points"; that is where the tally marks go. For each bulletin you read, put down a tally mark beside yours or your partner's name. If you read a statement that so happens to describe you and you want to work on that area, then write it down under your strengths and weaknesses. If you find a statement on the list that describes you, and it may be something that your partner always complains about, then write it down as well. Once you're done, work on these areas together so that you guys can build a healthier relationship.

Part 4: Particular Roles Played in a Relationship

SCORE SHEET

Participant 1

Name: ______________________________
Date: __________________
Age: ____________

Strengths:

____

____

____

____

____

____

Weaknesses:

____

____

____

____

____

____

____

____

Total Points:

____

____

SCORE SHEET

Participant 2

Name: ______________________________
Date: __________________
Age: ____________

Strengths:

____

____

____

____

____

____

Weaknesses:

____

____

____

____

____

____

____

____

Total Points:

____

____

Particular Roles Played in a Relationship

The Planner

• You put all the events and entertainment together in the relationship such as date nights, going to the movies, church events, and etc.
• Your partner depends on your advice when it comes to planning things.
• You keep the relationship steady.

The Organizer

• You focus better when organized and on time.
• You keep things in order.
• Everything has to be neat and clean.
• You have a set schedule that you live by.
• You feel off-track if you don't go by your schedule.

Money

• You are the spender in the relationship.
• You help finance the relationship.
• You are in charge of the money.
• You pay for all the date nights.
• You feel like you always have to help pay for everything.
• Your partner treats you like an ATM.
• Your partner is a shopaholic.

Time Management

• You are the organized person in the relationship

• You keep everything on a timely schedule.

• You manage everything in the relationship.

• Being on time is important to you.

• You don't like to be late.

• There's a conflict in the relationship when your partner doesn't go by your set schedule.

The Oven Glove

• You have to carry the heat of different things inside the relationship.

• You have to handle all of the hard stuff.

• Your partner is difficult to deal with at times.

• Your partner is argumentative.

• Your partner is willing do things on purpose to hurt you or to upset you.

The Lemon

• Your partner has a bad attitude.

• You are the one who is always dealing with the sour taste of your relationship.

• You always have to bite your tongue.

• You always apologize to save the relationship.

• Every day you have a sour attitude.

The Toilet Bowl Brush

- You feel like you always get the dirty jobs in the relationship.
- You are the one who always cleans up.
- You have to deal with the messy jobs.
- You cook the meals.
- You do the dirty laundry.
- You work long hours.
- Your partner never cleans up after themselves.

The Knife

- Iron sharpens iron.
- You cut out all of the negative things and help sharpen the relationship and get everything back in order.
- You are the thinker in the relationship.
- You cut off the unnecessary things.
- Your words can either sharpen someone or cut them.

The Bandage

- You cover up the pain that's on the out-side and hide it inside.
- You don't show any emotions.
- For years, you been dealing with the same stuff, and you feel like you've been keeping that part of your life silent for way too long.

The Pain Ointment

- You always get hurt by your partner physically, mentally, or emotionally.
- You're always trying to fix stuff in the relationship, so you deal with the pain alone.
- You keep the things from your past relationship bottled up inside, and it has been affecting your new relationship.

The Mirror or the Magnifying Glass

- The natural mirror is the real you.
- The magnifying glass is when the person is different the next day.
- You always change things around in the relationship.
- Dating a person that's a magnifying glass is difficult because you never know what you're going to get.

The Weightlifter

- You are the stronger one in the relationship.
- You have to carry the whole load alone.
- You pay all the bills.
- You keep gas in the car.
- You keep the relationship financially stable.

The Newspaper

• Your future spouse doesn't take you seriously at all.
• You are the messenger in the relationship.
• You have to give out all the good news.
• You have to give out all the bad news.
• Your partner treats you like a joke.
• Your partner is overloaded with ideas.
• Your partner has bad communication skills.
• Your partner is a bad listener and doesn't know how to communicate with you.

The Garbage Disposal

• Your partner treats you like trash.
• They throw everything on you.
• Their words cut you.
• They see you as less than what you really are.
• They talk trash to you.
• They have a filthy mouth.
• Their lifestyle is unclean.
• They hold on to dead things.
• They collect waste such as past arguments, past failures, old relationship, etc.

Date: ____________________

NOTES

____

____

____

____

____

____

____

____

____

____

____

____

____

____

____

____

____

____

____

____

____

"And Jacob served seven years for Rachel; and they seemed unto him but a few days, for the love he had to her."
Genesis 29:20

Chapter 7

†

How to Balance a Godly Relationship While Operating in Ministry

"And let us consider one another to provoke unto love and to good works: Not forsaking the assembling of ourselves together, as the manner of some is; but exhorting one another: and so much the more, as ye see the day approaching." Hebrews 10:24-25

Courting While Operating in Ministry

2 Peter 3:18 says, "But grow in grace, and in the knowledge of our Lord and Saviour Jesus Christ. To him be glory both now and for ever. Amen." God allows us to have fellowship with other believers through courtship, so when you are court-

ing other believers in Christ, make sure that it is ordained by God. Many Christian believers have wasted so much time with people who God has not destined them to be with. Sometimes watching other peers court and get married can make you feel left out, unwanted, and alone. Loneliness can cause the devil to creep in and send someone as a distraction to get you off-balance. The devil knows what captures your attention, so he will try to send people in your life as a hindrance to stop you from doing what God has called you to do.

How will you know if they are a distraction from Satan? You will begin to lose focus on your God-given assignment, everything will become overwhelming to you, and you will begin to lose interest in doing the things of God. That's when you have to pray and ask God if they are the future spouse that He desires for you to have. After praying, if you begin to realize that they were not sent by God, then repent and ask Him to remove this person out of your life graciously. How will you know if they're God-sent? Well, God will begin to show you that this is the person that He is allowing you to date. So, don't allow your loneliness to distract you from your purpose because, in due season, God will send someone who He has designed just for you. In conclusion, if you want a successful relationship while you are operating in ministry, you have to remain focused on God, stay on course with your God-given assignment, and continue to allow God to be in full control of the relationship.

How to Balance a Godly Relationship While Operating in Ministry

Job 31:6 says, "Let me be weighed in an even balance that God may know mine integrity." God has a vision for your life, and He has called you to do great things in ministry. Sometimes, it can be quite challenging trying to balance out a relationship and ministry all at the same time. Due to our jobs, busy schedules, and other obligations, it can become difficult to make time for your partner. This next session will teach you how to balance out common things that you may face while courting in ministry.

Sometimes believers can forget that other than ministry, they have mates, marriages, or families. Some people don't know how to balance everything out. By doing this, it can cause some friction within their relationships. Some may feel that their partners can't ever make time for them. Others may feel that the church is occupying all of their partners' time and attention. When you are operating in ministry, the best way to balance out a godly relationship is to make God the main focus of the relationship. Make Him the main substance that you need to help your relationship grow in Him. When you are courting in ministry, use God as a foundation, use the Word of God as a source, and use your prayer life to sustain your relationship. Once you do this, ask God to give you instructions on how to spend some quality time with your partner without withdrawing from ministry.

As God teaches you how to make time for your partner, show them that you care about their companionship even though you have a position at your local church. Show them that their time is more valuable to you just like it is to the church. Make sure that they understand that no matter how much time you may spend with them, their time will never be more important than what God is requiring for you to do in ministry. Always remind them that their time is important to you, but God has a higher demand for you, so therefore He requires all of your time.

Make Sure Your Relationship Stays Sacred Before God

Deuteronomy 29:29 says, "The secret things belong unto the Lord our God: but those things which are revealed belong unto us and to our children for ever, that we may do all the words of this law." When you hold a position in the church, it is to help edify the body of Christ. Therefore, everything that you do in ministry should be sacred unto God. Another form of being sacred unto God is being clean. Cleanliness is godliness, so anyone who holds a title in the church should stay in cleanliness. Cleanliness is the state or quality of being clean or being kept clean. Leviticus 10:10 (ESV) says, "You are to distinguish between the holy and the common, and between the unclean and the clean..." God isn't going to dwell in an unclean temple, so you have to keep a clean lifestyle.

When you are dating while operating in ministry, you want to do things that will be pleasing in God's eyes. You have to allow God's character to be shown through you. When God's light is shining in your life, you will have those who will be attracted to it. For this cause, some of the saints will be watching your lifestyle very closely. You will have those who will be looking at your character and how you carry yourself as a Christian. Meanwhile, you have to be careful of the things that you may do in front of the people of God because you never want anyone's soul to be in damnation because of your sin. If you want to display a godly relationship, you have to keep your relationship sacred before God.

Here are some steps on how to date in secrecy.

Step #1: Keep your relationship pure.

Make sure that you and your partner remain in purity while dating.

Step #2: Never practice ungodly deeds while you are dating.

God reviews all things, whether they are good or bad. So, you have to be careful of the things you may do or say in front of others.

Step #3: Don't condone sinful acts.

Most people who love sin will look for excuses to sin. While courting in ministry, don't act in any way that will cause others to fall for temptation. You never know who's watching you, so don't be the cause of someone falling because they are watching your lifestyle too closely.

Step #4: Set a good example by being a godly example.

Maintain a godly relationship by praying and asking God to teach you and your partner how to set an image that will be Christ-like that won't lead the people of God astray.

2 Corinthians 4:2 (ESV) says, "But we have renounced disgraceful, underhanded ways. We refuse to practice cunning or to tamper with God's word, but by the open statement of the truth we would commend ourselves to everyone's conscience in the sight of God."

"Your relationship has to be built on honesty because if it's built on false pretenses, it's not going to last. Sometimes, in a relationship, they need to see the real you."
-Mitchell Brooks (my father)

Communication is the Key

- Talk about it.
- Lay it all out on the table.
- Have trust.
- Have stability.
- Stay true to your word.
- Use kind words towards one another.
- Tell your partner how much you admire them.
- Keep negative people out of your business.
- Hear each other out.
- Apologize if you make a mistake.
- Focus on the concerns of you partner.
- Set goals for the relationship.
- Date to fall in love.
- Be wise of ungodly counsel.
- Don't bring outsiders with negative opinions into your relationship.
- Don't act on everything that you hear about your partner.
- Don't gossip about your mate.
- It's ok to have mutual disagreements, but don't purposely embarrass your partner in

front of others.

• Everything that you and your mate may discuss privately shouldn't be discuss publicly.

• Show your partner how much you care about them with your actions and not just your words.

Date: ____________________

NOTES

____
____
____
____
____
____
____
____
____
____
____
____
____
____
____
____
____
____
____
____
____
____

"And let us not be weary in well doing: for in due season we shall reap, if we faint not."
Galatians 6:9

Chapter 8

†

No Sex Zone

"Now concerning the things whereof ye wrote unto me: It is good for a man not to touch a woman. Nevertheless, to avoid fornication, let every man have his own wife, and let every woman have her own husband."
1 Corinthians 7:1-2

No-Sex Zone

1 Corinthians 7:5 says, "Defraud ye not one the other, except it be with consent for a time, that ye may give yourselves to fasting and prayer; and come together again, that Satan tempt you not for your incontinency." 1 Corinthians 7:32 says, "But I would have you without carefulness. He that is unmarried careth for the things that belong to

the Lord, how he may please the Lord..." How can we please the Lord? There are many biblical verses in the Bible that teach us how to do things that will be pleasing in God's eyes. Well, did you know that serving God in purity is a form of pleasing Him? Another way to please Him is through saving yourself from sexual intercourse. Once you become a Christian, you have to realize that you were bought with a price and your body is not your own. Therefore, you have to learn how to keep yourself in purity while you are waiting to get married. The purpose for this chapter is to help Christian men and women save themselves for marriage. As a young believer in Christ, I realized that there is a lack in teaching Christians how to abstain from sex until their spouse comes. Many people have shared with me how hard it is to save yourself once you start dating. So, I decided to share some great tips for those who are desiring to abstain from sex while courting. Hopefully, these tips will be useful for you and your partner so you guys can live in celibacy. Also, for those of you who are single and desiring to commit yourself to purity, then I would like to share with you how God can keep you while you are abstaining yourself from sex. 1 Thessalonians 4:3 says, "For this is the will of God, even your sanctification, that ye should abstain from fornication..."

My Body is the Temple of the Holy Spirit

1 Corinthians 6:19-20 (AMP) says, "Do you not know that your body is a temple of the Holy Spirit who is within you, whom you have [received as a gift] from God, and that you are not your own [property]? You were bought with a price [you were actually purchased with the precious blood of Jesus and made His own]. So then, honor and glorify God with your body."

Did you know that your body is the property of the Holy Spirit? Do you know that you were bought with a price? So, how can we as Christians learn how to avoid fornication if we don't know how valuable our bodies are to the Holy Spirit? Sometimes it can be quite difficult to avoid premarital sex if you don't know how to abstain while you are in a relationship. While you are dating, how will you and your partner honor God with your bodies? Will you be able to flee from temptation if the opportunity were to present itself? 1 Corinthians 6:19-20 tells us how to honor God with our body by glorifying Him with it.

The following sections will teach couples how to abstain from premarital sex by glorifying God with their bodies, abstaining from sexual desires, and how to remain in purity while courting. At the end of this chapter, I will give out some great tips that will help teach couples how to avoid fornication while dating.

Glorify God with Your Body

How do you glorify God with your body? Do you submit to sexual immoralities, or do you offer your body up to God as a sacrifice by remaining in purity? When you begin to understand that your body is not your own because it's the temple of the Holy Spirit, then you will know how to save yourself for marriage. Yes, God did design our bodies to procreate and reproduce, but your body is to remain sacred unto God for your spouse. So, why is glorifying God with our bodies so important? Because there is such a demand for us to keep our bodies holy unto God. The keys to honoring God with your body are to remain celibate, give Him thanks, worship Him in spirit and in truth, and obey His commands about avoiding fornication. Other ways to glorify God with your body are by studying the Word, staying in purity, and setting a godly example for unbelievers.

1 Thessalonians 4:1-7 (AMP) says, "Finally, believers, we ask and admonish you in the Lord Jesus, that you follow the instruction that you received from us about how you ought to walk and please God (just as you are actually doing) and that you excel even more and more [pursuing a life of purpose and living in a way that expresses gratitude to God for your salvation]. For you know what commandments and precepts we gave you by the authority of the Lord Jesus.

For this is the will of God, that you be sanctified [separated and set apart from sin]: that you abstain and back away from sexual immorality; that each of you know how to control his own body in holiness and honor [being available for God's purpose and separated from things profane], not [to be used] in lustful passion, like the Gentiles who do not know God and are ignorant of His will; and that [in this matter of sexual misconduct] no man shall transgress and defraud his brother because the Lord is the avenger in all these things, just as we have told you before and solemnly warned you. For God has not called us to impurity, but to holiness [to be dedicated, and set apart by behavior that pleases Him, whether in public or in private]."

How to Abstain from Sexual Desires

Live in celibacy! When you are living in celibacy, you have to rededicate your body unto God and not operate in any sexual intercourse until marriage. For those who don't desire to get married, then they have to ask Jesus Christ to come into their hearts and make them celibate so they can live for Him. If you want God to be pleased with you, then you will have to learn how to walk away from sexual temptations. When you are dating someone, walking away from premarital sex is not easy, but you don't want your soul to go to hell for committing any sexual sins. 1 Corinthians 7:9 (ESV) teaches us, "But if they cannot exercise self-control, they should marry. For it is better to marry than to burn with passion." Once you read this scripture, if you realized that you cannot exercise self-control, then pray and ask God to teach you how to do so.

Next, how will you be able to abstain from sexual desires? Many may say through praying–and yes, that's true. But I've learned that when you are trying to remain in purity, you have to ask God to help you subdue the passion for sex. Subduing the passion means asking God to help you go without sex until your spouse comes. Once you start dedicating your body to Him, then He will teach you how to save your body for marriage. Hebrews 13:4 says, "Marriage is honourable in all, and the bed undefiled: but whoremongers and adulterers God will judge."

Also, I've learned that there is power in prayer. So, when you are praying about your sexual desires, you never want to ask God to take your desire for sex away. The reason why is because one day you will get married, and if you pray for things such as this, then one day you will find yourself losing the desire to have sex with your partner. That's why it's so important to ask God to subdue the passion. Meaning: take the desire away for that moment. 1 Peter 4:19 says,

"Wherefore let them that suffer according to the will of God commit the keeping of their souls to him in well doing, as unto a faithful Creator."

In other words, ask God to remove anything out of your life that will try to cause you to commit any sexual deeds that go against Him or His Word. Once you start praying for things such as this, the devil will try to tempt you. That's when you have to pray and ask God to help you sustain yourself so you can avoid fornication. 1 John 2:15-17 says, "Love not the world, neither the things that are in the world. If any man love the world, the love of the Father is not in him. For all that is in the world, the lust of the flesh, and the lust of the eyes, and the pride of life, is not of the Father, but is of the world. And the world passeth away, and the lust thereof: but he that doeth the will of God abideth for ever."

Therefore, if you are struggling with any sexual immoralities such as porn addiction, the spirit of perversion, or any lustful spirits that cause you to act out of the will of God, then you need to repent and ask God to forgive you for your sins. Doing this allows Him to take away any lustful desires that you may have been battling with. Once you do this, rededicate your body unto God and start living in purity.

Remain Holy in Purity

Live by the spirit and not by the flesh. For the fleshly man desires things that the spirit doesn't desire. I heard my pastor once say this: "God doesn't bless your fleshly desires of lust. So, don't allow your flesh to get your soul in trouble with God." Romans 8:1, 5, 8, and 10 say, "There is therefore now no condemnation to them which are in Christ Jesus, who walk not after the flesh, but after the Spirit...For they that are after the flesh do mind the things of the flesh; but they that are after the Spirit the things of the Spirit... So then they that are in the flesh cannot please God...And if Christ be in you, the body is dead because of sin; but the Spirit is life because of righteousness." You Christian believers who are courting should know that if you remain in purity, then it will always keep your body Holy unto God. 1 Corinthians 7:32 (ESV) says, "I want you to be free from anxieties. The unmarried man is anxious about the things of the Lord, how to please the Lord." If you want to please the Lord with your body, then remain in purity.

TIPS: How to Avoid Fornication

- Remain in purity.
- Stay celibate.
- Ask God to help you save yourself for your spouse and marriage.

• You can be romantic without having sex.
• Don't put yourself in a predicament that will cause you to fall in the hands of temptation.
• Avoid French kissing. (Sometimes kissing can lead to sex.)
• Avoid sexual conversations and topics about sex.
• Don't touch each other in inappropriate places.
• Don't have oral sex.
• Avoid watching movies, TV shows, or music videos that have sexual content in them.
• Don't spend time alone with your partner if you are not strong-minded enough to say "no" to premarital sex.
• Don't spend the night at your partner's house. (This will help you avoid kissing, touching, or committing fornication.)
• Don't do seductive dances for your partner. This can strike a mood if they are not strong-minded. Doing this will help them avoid hav ing lustful thoughts about your body.
• When you feel yourself getting sexually aroused, pray and ask God to help you stay sanctified in Him through purification.
• When you feel tempted to have premarital sex with your partner, one way to prevent it from happening is by reading the Bible with your partner. Doing this will help you keep

your mind focused on God.

- If your partner so happens to turn you on, then allow God to turn you off. Ask Him to subdue your passion for sex for that moment.
- It's okay to cuddle with your partner; just don't lay on them in inappropriate ways.
- Don't be a pervert by having a lustful eye for everything that crosses your path.
- Don't be seductive with your partner by showing them your body parts.
- Don't expose your body parts by wearing in appropriate clothing.
- Don't take inappropriate pictures (ex. exposing your body or sharing flirtatious poses).
- Don't send inappropriate videos to your partner.
- Unless there's a conflict with your work schedule that prevents you from seeing your partner during the daytime, try not to meet them at night. This will help you avoid temptations such as spending the night or fornicating.
- Don't have multiple sex partners before or after marriage. This will prevent you and your partner from catching sexually transmitted diseases.
- Don't watch porn; it's a sin. Watching porn with your partner will stir up some feelings

that you cannot control. Don't allow the devil to use that as a weapon to cause you to fornicate.

- Don't masturbate; it's a sin. Masturbation is a sexual desire that causes you to give your body self-pleasure. It invites in the spirit of perversion that will open the door to allow other demonic spirits to come into your home or your body. Ephesians 5:11 says, "And have no fellowship with the unfruitful works of darkness, but rather reprove them."

Note: Repent if you have done anything that was on this list. Ask God to help you stay holy unto Him and to help you change your lifestyle for the better. Learn how to avoid fornication by resisting the devil and his temptations. If there is anyone in your life who doesn't agree with you living by this list, then remove them from your life so that you can remain in purity.

Activities that You Can Do with Your Partner to Help You Avoid Fornication

- Read the Bible together.
- Read a book.
- Use that energy somewhere else.
- Go work out as a couple.
- Go for a run.
- Go on a date.

- Go to the movies.
- Visit a nice restaurant. Go somewhere elegant and fancy.
- Go bowling.
- Go to the skating rink.
- Go to a concert together such as a church event, a Gospel Explosion, or a musical.
- Go to see a famous gospel artist.
- Go to the boardwalk.
- Go play games at the arcade.
- Go to the mall.
- Go shopping.
- Share some ice cream together.
- Plan a trip to Dave and Busters.
- Go swimming or plan a trip to a water park.
- Plan a turnaround trip to Six Flags or an amusement park. Go and come back the same day.
- Buy some crawfish or shrimp and go sit at a park and eat it. Then, push each other on a swing.
- Go on a picnic date in your backyard or at your local park.

Prayer: Avoiding Fornication

1 Corinthians 6:18 (ESV) says, "Flee from sexual immorality. Every other sin a person commits is outside the body, but the sexually immoral person sins against his own body."

Dear Heavenly Father,

I come to You through Your Son Jesus's name, asking for forgiveness. This chapter exposed a lot of hidden secrets that many people may battle with privately. Throughout the chapter, we have found some traits that showed us our true character. If we want lifestyles that will please and honor You, help us flee from any sexual temptation. While we're courting our partners, teach us how to abstain from premarital sex. Continue to teach us how to glorify You with our bodies. When we have moments when we feel like we're experiencing sexual arousal, then we will pray to You and ask You to subdue the passion for sex for that moment. Today, we're asking You to forgive us for committing any sexual immoralities of lust. We bind up any demonic spirits of lust, pornography, masturbation, or lustful pleasures of this world. We command these spirits to leave our bodies and homes in the mighty name of Jesus. Lustful spirits, be gone and don't return! God, from this day forward, give me the strength to walk away from the things that could cause me to lust after the flesh. Colossians 3:1-8 (ESV) says, "If then you have been raised with Christ, seek the things that are above, where Christ is, seated at the right hand of God. Set your minds on things that are above, not on things that are on earth. For you have died, and your life is hidden with Christ in God. When Christ who is your life appears, then you also will appear with him in glory. Put to death therefore what is earthly in you: sexual immorality, impurity, passion, evil desire, and covetousness, which is idolatry. On account of these the wrath of God is coming. In these you too once walked, when you were living in them. But now you must put them all away..."

God, I do recognize that I can no longer fornicate or commit any sexual deeds because it goes against Your Word. So, today I will continue to remain in purity until my spouse comes. God, keep me when I can't keep myself. That way, I am always covered by Your blood.

In Jesus' name I pray. Amen!

Date: ____________________

NOTES

____
____
____
____
____
____
____
____
____
____
____
____
____
____
____
____
____
____
____
____
____

"Nevertheless let every one of you in particular so love his wife even as himself; and the wife see that she reverence her husband."
Ephesians 5:33

Chapter 9

†

No Same-Sex Marriages

"Thou shalt not lie with mankind, as with womankind: it is abomination." Leviticus 18:22

James 4:7 says, "Submit yourselves therefore to God. Resist the devil, and he will flee from you."

Why do people become gay and turn to an alternative lifestyle?

- Rape
- "Tomboy" label growing up
- Love issues
- Neglect as children from their mothers and/or fathers

- Relationship problems
Hurt by someone in a relationship
- Weariness from dating the opposite sex
- Giving in to peer pressure
- Feeling like they were born that way
- Not being attracted to the opposite sex
- Being forced into that lifestyle
- Watching pornography or watching gay porn growing up
- Having same-sex parents
- Feeling dominant / Playing the role of the opposite sex
- Being introduced to it at a young age
- Liking dressing up in the opposite sex's clothes (ex. boys wearing girls' clothing)
- Having gay friends
- Enjoying engaging in gay sex
- Not knowing their true identity
- Feeling comfortable being gay
- Wanting to be free being themselves
-Feeling that being gay allows them to express their true identity by dating the same sex. (It's a form of freedom for them.)

No Same-Sex Marriages: Part 1

Romans 1:26-28 says, "For this cause God gave them up unto vile affections: for even their women did change the natural use into that which is against nature: And likewise also the men, leaving the natural use of the woman, burned in their lust one toward another; men with men working that which is unseemly, and receiving in themselves that recompence of their error which was meet. And even as they did not like to retain God in their knowledge, God gave them over to reprobate mind, to do those things which are not convenient..."

We as Christians are so quick to judge people without finding out why they live in an alternative lifestyle. How can we help these people get delivered? How can we help them turn away from sin and give their lives back unto Jesus Christ? 2 Chronicles 7:14 says, "If my people, which are called by my name, shall humble themselves, and pray, and seek my face, and turn from their wicked ways; then will I hear from heaven, and will forgive their sin, and will heal their land."

In this chapter, I will discuss why same-sex couples should not get married. Through research, biblical studies, and observations, I have learned that it is a demonic spirit that causes the individual to like the same sex. My job is not to condemn those who may live in this alternative lifestyle but to bring forth correction so that they may change their lifestyles and serve the Lord. Also, I would like to inform you that just because I don't agree with the LGBTQ community, it doesn't mean that I hate or dislike them. I just don't condone their lifestyle choices. I still love them because God is love. However, as a Christian, I have to remember that God loves the person. He just hates the sin. Galatians 5:14 says, "For all the law is fulfilled in one word, even in this; Thou shalt love thy neighbour as thyself."

Understanding the True Meaning of Homosexuality

The term "gay" came from homosexual men. This is a way for them to describe their sexual orientation. Gay is a term that primarily refers to a homosexual person or the state of being a homosexual. Homosexuality is when two people of the same sex try to join together as one. What does the Bible say about homosexuality? Leviticus 18:22 says, "Thou shalt not lie with mankind, as with womankind: it is abomination." Leviticus 20:13 says, "If a man also lie with mankind, as he lieth with a woman, both of them have committed an abomination: they shall surely be put to death; their blood shall be upon them." A "detestable" act is an act that is an abomination to the Lord. When you reflect on the term "abomination", it is a thing that causes disgust or hatred, which is exceptionally loathsome, hateful, sinful, wicked, or vile. Deuteronomy 22:5 says, "The woman shall not wear that which pertaineth unto a man, neither shall a man put on a woman's garment: for all that do so are abomination unto the Lord thy God."

Same-Sex Attractions

I believe that those who are in love with the same sex battle with same-sex attraction. People who battle with this spirit will seek spiritual direction for various reasons. Some seek direction to help them understand their same-sex feelings or preferences. Many others seek guidance in other aspects of life to help them find their true identity. Most of these people like to pick the gender that they feel that they were born with. This brings on a confused spirit. This spirit has deceived the person into believing that they were born one way, but God created them differently than their true gender. 1 John 4:1 (ESV) says, "Beloved, do not believe every spirit, but test the spirits to see whether they are from God, for many false prophets have gone out into the world." If a person battles with knowing their true sexual identity, then they will have to turn back unto God and ask Him to show them who they really are in Christ. Isaiah 45:22 says, "Look unto me, and be ye saved, all the ends of the earth: for I am God, and there is none else."

Battling with an Identity Crisis

For those of you who may not know, LGBTQ stands for "Lesbians, Gays, Bisexuals, Transgendered, and Questioning". Although this community has their own beliefs and preferences about their sexuality, I would like to share my own God-given perspective on this topic. I feel that those who are in the LGBTQ community battle with the spirit of homosexuality. I believe that this lifestyle has a cause, and it affects the way that they have chosen to live their lives. So, why is there such a big fuss about being gay or coming out? Why do people of this community turn to an alternative lifestyle? Most of these people are afraid to share why they turn to the same sex because they are fearful of what society may think of them. I feel that many of these people have personal battles that they may face that society doesn't know about. People who struggle with coming out face depression, self-harm, and suicidal thoughts. They feel like no one accepts, understands, or knows their true identity.

So, how can we get those who are part of the LGBT community to know their true identity in Christ? How can we show them the love of Christ without condemning them for their sins? Easy. You have to learn how to accept the person that God has called them to be and not what the person has preferred or chosen to be recognized as. Once you begin to recognize their identity in Christ, then God will begin to do a marvelous work in their life. 1 Thessalonians 2:13 (ESV) says, " And we also thank God constantly for this, that when you received the word of God, which you heard from us, you accepted it not as the word of men but as what it really is, the word of God, which is at work in you believers."

Dating The Same Sex

Most relationships require couples to have signs of love and affection such as kissing, hugging, providing, and being supportive toward one another. When it comes to couples dating the same sex, they expect to do the same thing that regular couples would do. Most gay couples want the same rights as straight couples. Some believe that if they are not given the same rights or treatment that are given to heterosexual couples, then they are being subjected to sexual discrimination. Sexual discrimination is sexism, prejudice, or discrimination based on a person's sex or gender. Sexism can affect anyone, but it primarily affects women and girls on a systematic level. It has been linked to stereotypes and gender roles and may include the belief that one sex or gender is intrinsically superior to another.

Many people in the LGBTQ community believe that when it comes to getting married, a lot of people disagree with them marrying the same sex. I read a study once that stated if people of the same sex were to get married, then it would violate one of God's most important laws called the "law of chastity". The law of chastity applies to both men and women. It includes strict abstinence from sexual relations before marriage and complete fidelity and loyalty to one's spouse after marriage.

The law of chastity requires that sexual relations be reserved for marriage between a man and a woman. If a man or woman of the same sex breaks this law, then it will be an unsacred ceremony that will get in the way of their eternal progress. If you break this law, the only way that you can be reconciled with God is through repentance. Part two of this chapter will focus on same-sex marriages and why it has such a big effect in today's society.

Part 2: No Same-Sex Marriage

Same-sex marriage is the practice of marriage between two men or two women. Although same-sex marriage has been regulated through law, religion, and custom in most countries of the world, the legal and social responses have ranged from celebration on the one hand to criminalization on the other. American law allows same-sex couples to have civil or religious ceremonies that join them together through marriage. (Reference: https://www.britannica.com/topic/same-sex-marriage)

One big question in today's society is: "Will same-sex marriages confuse the younger generation?" Well, I believe I have an answer to this question. I read a study once that had been focused on younger children. The study involved getting children's point of view about same-sex marriage. The primary question they set out to answer was: "Will approving same-sex marriages confuse the children of this generation?" The psychologist who did the study allowed each child to watch a video promoting gay rights and same-sex marriage proposals. After the psychologist tested their hypothesis, it showed that each age group had different opinions about the topic. I would like to take a moment to share this study with you. The first study was called "Men to Men". The age group "6 to 7 years" didn't understand why a man proposed to another man. The age group "12 to 13 years" thought it was okay, cute, and sweet. One child in this age group felt that the whole video was wrong. She said that men shouldn't be with men but instead should marry women.

The second study was called: "Women to Women". The age group "6 to 7 years" still didn't understand why a woman proposed to a woman like in the "Man to Man" study. When it came to gay rights, the older children agreed that gay people should be together. Many of them stated that they wanted to see more proposals like this in the future. One child still didn't like the fact that men and women of the same sex were proposing to their same-sex partners. During the video, some of the children even stated that they were born gay and this was a sign of freedom for them. Although the younger kids thought that being gay was bad, the older kids thought that it was a good thing. By the end of the video, fourteen out of fifteen children were agreeing with same-sex marriages.

Here are my thoughts and beliefs: the older the child gets, the more the world tries to make the child understand that it is okay to be gay. It's okay that men marry men – same with women marrying women. Society wants us to think that this is the new normal. They make movies, TV shows, and songs about being gay so that we can become comfortable with gay rights. But in all reality, this is wrong! God is displeased with it. 1 Corinthians 6:9-10 (ESV) says, "Or do you not know that the unrighteous will not inherit the kingdom of God? Do not be deceived: neither the sexually immoral, nor idolaters, nor adulterers, nor men who practice homosexuality, nor thieves, nor the greedy, nor drunkards, nor revilers, nor swindlers will inherit the kingdom of God."

Furthermore, the Lord told me that He doesn't approve of same-sex marriages. He reminded me of the stories of Sodom and Gomorrah and how He destroyed their land because of their wickedness and sin. Genesis 19:13 (ESV) says, "For we are about to destroy this place, because the outcry against its people has become great before the Lord, and the Lord has sent us to destroy it." The Lord continued to tell me, "When somebody gets married to the same sex, that is something that was approved by Man and not by God." He stated this: "I will not approve or condone something that goes against Me or My Word." He also emphasized, "Marriage should only be done by a man and a woman." The Holy Spirit told me His definition of marriage. He said, "Marriage is a covenant that a man and a woman make before God and the Church. It is a sacred ceremony that should not be played with or taken for granted." Ephesians 5:25-26 says, "Husbands, love your wives, even as Christ also loved the church, and gave himself for it; That he might sanctify and cleanse it with the washing of water by the word..."

Nowadays, mankind approves of anything. The things that God rejects, Man approves of, and the things that He approves of, Man rejects. When you are living in an alternative lifestyle, please quit trying to get Man's approval for everything because their decision will cost you your salvation in the end. When you look up the term "salvation", it's deliverance from sin and its consequences, believed by Christians to be brought about by faith in Christ. If you are an unbeliever or a person who is operating in sin, God will deliver you from those things only if you have faith and believe that He can do it.

Part 3: No Same-Sex Marriages

When I was attending Southern University, my English class was required to write an essay about an experiment that we did on fellow peers on campus. This experiment required us to test a theory on a topic that we might disagree on, but we had to have evidence to prove that the results from our experiment were valid. After doing hours of research, I decided to do my essay on the LGBTQ community. I took it upon myself to interview different students around the campus to see why they chose to live an alternative lifestyle. It was called "A Study on Gay People's Point of View about Same-Sex Marriage". I personally interviewed seven different students to get their perspectives on same-sex marriages.

After my interviews were over, I had to prove to my class that the knowledge I had gained from doing research and studying fellow students was accurate. After presenting my results to the class, I had to prove that the information that was given to them was right. In this section, I will give the same details that I gave to my class during my presentation. Every statement that follows is from prior interviews that

I conducted with the students around campus.

Each interview was done in a separate location because I didn't want anyone's answers to be influenced or persuaded by outside people's opinions. Many of the students I interviewed stated that their sexuality was changed based on past experiences that they had as children that caused them to live the lifestyles that they have chosen today. Most of these individuals are Christians. and they know that it's wrong to be a homosexual or lesbian, but they have chosen this lifestyle instead and despite the consequence that comes with it. For brevity, I will only share four of my interviews.

Also, no confidential information such as real names, addresses, or locations will be shared as they pertain to this experiment so that all students' identities can be kept private and confidential. After my theory and experiment were presented, I offered those who desired it to be delivered a prayer of salvation called "A Prayer for Deliverance". This prayer allowed God to come in and change their lives because this lifestyle does require a change. Down below are studies, research, and interviews that I did on students at my formal college.

INTERVIEW: QUESTIONS & ANSWERS GAY PEOPLE'S POINT OF VIEW ABOUT SAME-SEX MARRIAGE

Question #1: "What attracts you to another man?"

Interviewee #1 (Male) Responses:

- He has to be masculine.
- He has to choose to be the dominant person in the relationship.

Interviewee #2 (Male) Responses:

- Their energy attracts me to them.
- Their appearance– if I see a resemblance of me in that person.
- It's a natural thing; it's the way he speaks to you as a man compared to how a woman does.

Interviewee #3 (Male) Responses:

- His goal is to attract a male that is very masculine with a nice body who has trust and honesty.
- He also wants someone who will allow him to be himself without changing him into something that he's not.

Interviewee #4 (Female) Responses:

- It's their smile and their beauty.
- I am not attracted to men or what they have

to offer, but I do like dating women and what they have to offer.

Question #2: "Do you think being gay will bring confusion to the younger generation?"

Interviewee #1 (Male) Response:

- "Yes because the child will be confused with the two men sleeping together. And they are going to be confused about them being together."

Interviewee #2 (Male) Response:

- "Yes, I believe that the child will be confused, but I believe the child should be with whoever he loves. I would raise the child up to be straight, and that will be a choice they make on their own."

Interviewee #3 (Male) Response:

- "No because I feel like the child will not be affected by the situation. I don't believe that being gay will cause the child to want to be come gay, but I would tell them, 'this is the way that they have chosen to live their life.'"

Interviewee #4 (Female) Response:

- "Yes, it may confuse the child, but we will have to explain it to them."

Question #3: "What do your parents feel about your alternative lifestyle as a homosexual?"

Interviewee #1 (Male) Response:

- "It makes them cry and it also makes them feel ashamed about my lifestyle."

Interviewee #2 (Male) Response:

- "Different ways, some people can't stand or handle it and some people is cool with it."

Interviewee #3 (Male) Response:

- "It affected them to a certain degree, but at the end of the day the parents can teach their child the right way, but it's still the child's choice to become gay or not. Some people are closed-minded to the whole idea of homosexuality, but at the end of the day I chose to live in this lifestyle."

Interviewee #4 (Male) Response:

- "My mother didn't approve of my lifestyle, but my dad knew that I was going to become gay. But no one in my family judged me or looked at me differently."

Question #4: "Why do you believe that some men are gay?"

Interviewee #1 (Male) Response:

- "A spirit attached himself to him, which is a gay spirit."

Interviewee #2 (Male) Response:

- "Because I like boys, I enjoy doing feminine things. It's more of an attraction to a boy. And I feel like a woman is my best friend."

Interviewee #3 (Male) Response:

- "I believe that it affects some people differently. He chose to become gay because he realized that he's more attracted to male features than women. His ability to be himself and not to be ashamed about it."

Question #5: "Why do you believe that some women become gay?"

Interviewee #4 (Female) Response:

- "I always found girls more attractive to me than boys. I always liked girls more than I did with boys, anyway. Also, I never cared about anyone else's opinions about the way I lived my life. It's normal to be around someone for so long and begin to gain feelings for them."

Question #6: "Why do people of the same sex get married?"

Interviewee #1 (Male) Response:

- "Love, loyalty, and respect. Love causes a man and man to get married. And the fact that this person loves you and honors you, this causes you to want to marry them and support them."

Interviewee #2 (Male) Response:

- "It's the same thing as a straight person getting married. It will be that one person you will have feelings for that will make you love them and want to marry them. It's like a straight person getting married, but instead you are getting married to the same sex."

Interviewee #3 (Male) Response:

- Statement: Because of true and unconditional love. This person allows let you to be yourself around them.

Interviewee #4 (Female) Response:

- "I will comfort her in many ways. I would open the door for her, rub her feet when I come home from work, and I will take care of the household by paying all of the bills. If the connection that we have is strong then I think about marrying you. If we are together for some years and I have gained feelings for you then I will marry you. I feel like you should marry someone for the right reason and not for the wrong reasons."

Question #7: "How can two men of the same-sex teach a young girl how to become a woman?"

Interviewee #1 (Male) Response:

- "By observing my mother and sister, I learned how to deal with women. I will teach a girl how to become a woman by taking her around my grandmother, aunt, or girlfriend (girlfriend: girl that's a friend)."

Interviewee #2 (Male) Response:

- "They will use what they know from acting like a girl. A man will try his best to do what a woman does for her child. The child will still get the same love that they need. They will try to make the child comfortable about having them as a parent."

Interviewee #3 (Male) Response:

- "I will start by reminding her that she is beautiful, and I will give her confidence and love that she needs. As well as being a parent that walks in confidence in himself."

Question #8: "How can two women of the same sex raise up a boy and teach him how to become a man?"

Interviewee #4 (Female) Response:

- "First, I would toughen him up to make them tough as a man. Then, I would teach him how to be a gentleman. And I will also teach him how to treat a woman."

Question #9: "Do you think the lack of attention from your mother or father caused you to become gay?"

Interviewee #1 (Male) Response:

- "Yes because as a child in the fifth grade, I got less attention from my mother and father."

Interviewee #2 (Male) Response:

- "No, my mother accepts me living in this lifestyle."

Interviewee #3 (Male) Response:

- "Yes, it did because growing up as a child I was raised by my grandmother, and she taught me how to take care of myself if needed. Because it was just me and my sister, I had to play the role of a mother, I was taught the responsibility of a father, and I still had to be my sister's big brother at the end of the day. Because my mother was working all of the time, I had to play so many roles at such a young age. Now, since I have chosen to live an alternative lifestyle, this may not make sense to some people, but I believe this has an effect on how I live my life now. At the end of the day, I do understand that everyone has different opinions about the situation."

Interviewee #4 (Female) Response:

- "No because I was never attracted to boys, and I never wanted a boyfriend. I didn't want anything to do with them. I always liked girls more than boys, and I find them more attractive as well."

Question #10: "Do gay people get stereotyped in the workforce?"

Interviewee #1 (Male) Response:

- "No comment."

Interviewee #2 (Male) Response:

- "No, it doesn't bother me, but if a lot of people are staring at me, then I will just leave their presence."

Interviewee #3 (Male) Response:

- "No comment."

Interviewee #4 (Female) Response:

- "In some places, no, but in most places, yes. I feel like in most business places, they may prefer you to dress a certain way, but I feel like it shouldn't matter about that. It's about what you can bring to the table."

Question #11: "Were you born a homosexual?"

Answer: If you are engaging in homosexual activities, or believe that you are or were born a homosexual, I want to let you know that you were born the person that God called you to be. God did not call or ordain you to operate in the spirit of homosexuality. Jeremiah 1:5 says, "Before I formed thee in the belly I knew thee; and before thou camest forth out of the womb I sanctified thee."

Question #12: "Should people of the same sex get married?"

Answer: Leviticus 20:13 says, "If a man also lie with mankind, as he lieth with a woman, both of them have committed an abomination: they shall surely be put to death; their blood shall be upon them."

Question #13: "What should a man or a woman do when they have lost their attraction for the opposite sex?"

Answer: Pray and ask God to show them why they have lost their attraction for the opposite sex. Allow Him to show you the beauty in dating those of the opposite gender. Isaiah 50:9 (ESV) says, "Behold, the Lord helps me; who will declare me guilty? Behold, all of them will wear out like a garment; the moth will eat them up."

Question #14: "What do you do when you have a male who wants to be recognized as a Female or perhaps wants to be called 'ma'am' instead of 'sir'?"

Answer: You say, "Yes, dear, I do believe that you believe that, but according to my religion and belief, I cannot respect your wishes in calling you a name that is not of your gender. In honor of my Father in Heaven, I have to obey His Word and His commandments, and if you ask me to call you something that is out of the will of God, then that causes me to bring dishonor to my Father in Heaven."

Question #15: "What would happen if everyone in the world were to become a homosexual?"

Answer: It will be the end of human existence on the earth without medical intervention. The devil is trying to use this lifestyle to stop God's creation. Because without man and woman laying together in intimacy, they cannot have a child. By doing this, humanity will become extinct in one generation. Genesis 1:26-28 (MSG) says, "God spoke: 'Let us make human beings in our image, make them reflecting our nature So they can be responsible for the fish in the sea, the birds in the air, the cattle, And, yes, Earth itself, and every animal that moves on the face of Earth.' God created human beings; he created them godlike, Reflecting God's nature. He created them male and female. God blessed them..."'

Question #16: "What do you do when you want to change from living in an alternative lifestyle?"

Answer: God brings forth a change when He sees that you have humbled yourself to His spirit and are willing to submit yourself unto Him. Once you show Him that you desire a change, that's when a change will come. Ask God to deliver you from living an alternative lifestyle. That way, when temptation comes, you won't fall into the hands of the enemy. Psalm 107:6 (ESV) says, "Then they cried to the Lord in their trouble, and he delivered them from their distress." Galatians 5:1 says, "Stand fast therefore in the liberty wherewith Christ hath made us free, and be not entangled again with the yoke of bondage."

Part 4: Being Delivered from this Lifestyle and Obeying the Will of God

Living a homosexual lifestyle could be something that you have become accustomed to. You may have preferred this way of living over being straight for decades now. Maybe you are struggling with being transgendered, homosexual, or a lesbian, and you desire to be delivered from this spirit. Well, God sent His Son Jesus to die on the cross for our salvation. 1 John 1:9 (ESV) says, "If we confess our sins, he is faithful and just to forgive us our sins and to cleanse us from all unrighteousness." After reading this chapter, you may have realized that you no longer want to live in this lifestyle anymore. Maybe God has opened up your heart and soul so that He can change you and make you new. Well, today, I come to introduce you to a life that is worth living! This life is filled with everlasting life. John 10:10 says, "The thief cometh not, but for to steal, and to kill, and to destroy: I am come that they might have life, and that they might have it more abundantly." After submitting yourself to God, know that through Him, all of your old ways shall pass away, and God will make all things new in your life. Once you repent for your sins and actions, then God will come into your life and forgive you. Always remember that God's salvation is greater than your past. Follow these steps of transitioning so that you can become a new creature in Him.

Being Delivered & Becoming a New Creature in Christ

2 Corinthians 5:17 says, "Therefore if any man be in Christ, he is a new creature: old things are passed away; behold, all things are become new."

Step #1: Receive God as your Lord and Savior.
Step #2: Believe that He can deliver you.
Step #3: Accept the change that He will bring forth in your life.
Step #4: Be who God created you to be.
Step #5: Walk in the new you.
Step #6: Live life freely by avoiding sinful acts.
Step #7: Marry the opposite sex.
Step #8: Don't blame yourself for the things that you cannot control.
Step #9: Don't allow the devil to remind you of your past because God has already forgiven you for it.
Step #10: Read the Word of God daily.
Step #11: Stay Delivered.

A Prayer for Deliverance

1 John 5:4-5 (ESV) says, "For everyone who has been born of God overcomes the world. And this is the victory that has overcome the world—our faith. Who is it that overcomes the world except the one who believes that Jesus is the Son of God?"

Dear Heavenly Father,

I come to you in the mighty name of Jesus, confessing with my mouth and believing in my heart that God has raised Jesus from the dead and therefore I am saved. I repent for my sins, and I ask that You help me live a lifestyle that honors You. Lord, I am not asking You to help me condone sin but to take it away so that I may live and serve You. I ask that You reveal to me who I am in Christ. You said in 2 Corinthians 5:17 says, "Therefore if any man be in Christ, he is a new creature: old things are passed away; behold, all things are become new." Now that I know that I am a new creature, teach me the ways of Christ. Lord, we bind up any demonic spirit that tries to come against the image that You created me to be. Therefore, we cast down the spirit of homosexuality, transgenderism, and lesbianism in the mighty name of Jesus! I say it with authority that these spirits shall no longer have authority in my life in Jesus' name. I confess with my mouth that by the power of God, I am delivered and set free. Now that I have been delivered from these spirits, we bind Satan for trying to send those to remind me of my past.

Lord, if I have any past friends or people who I have fellowship with who approve of me living an alternative lifestyle, please remove them from my life. Father, it may be hard to let go of the ones I may love and adore, but if I want to spend eternity in Heaven with You, then I have to change my lifestyle. I will not walk in the spirit of disbelief, but I will walk in truth and by the Word of God. So, from this day forth, I will not be ashamed of my past, but I will witness to others about how God has delivered me and set me free from the spirit of homosexuality, transgenderism, or lesbianism. Father God, please keep me when I can't keep myself, and if You see me going astray, please catch me and hold me in Your loving arms. Father God, please don't let me die in sin, but allow me to live for You forever and always. In the mighty name of Jesus I pray, amen!

" For whosoever shall do the will of my Father which is in heaven, the same is my brother, and sister, and mother."
Matthew 12:50

Date: ____________________

NOTES

____

____

____

____

____

____

____

____

____

____

____

____

____

____

____

____

____

____

"If ye will fear the Lord, and serve him, and obey his voice, and not rebel against the commandment of the LORD, then shall both ye and also the king that reigneth over you continue following the Lord your God: But if ye will not obey the voice of the LORD, but rebel against the commandment of the Lord, then shall the hand of the Lord be against you, as it was against your fathers."
1 Samuel 12:14-15

Chapter 10

†

How to Carrry Yourself Until Your Spouse Comes

"Delight thyself also in the Lord: and he shall give thee the desires of thine heart."
Psalm 37:4

How to Carry Yourself Until Your Spouse Comes

• Study the Bible– God will begin to reveal Himself to you as you read the Word of God. When God shows you Himself through reading the Word, use that to your advantage. This will teach you what to look for in a person as you wait for your spouse. God is a good example of what you should wait for.

- Ladies, God has to prepare you for your husband. A "lady" is a woman of superior social position, especially one of noble birth. No matter the age, she is a beautiful female who has respect, morals, goals, ambition, and much more, one who knows what she deserves and knows how to be treated. One with much class on the outside but less class on the inside.
- Gentlemen, God has to prepare you for a wife. A "gentleman" is chivalrous, courteous, or honorable man; this is a polite or formal way of referring to a man.
- Know who you are in Christ.
- Carry yourself with class.
- Set high standards for yourself.
- Write down a list of traits that you admire about yourself.
- Dress to make a statement.
- Show your skills and things that you're good at.
- Your partner should be able to see characteristics that you are marriage material.
- You have to know your worth. Believe that you can have someone better than your past partner.
- Learn How to Be a Servant

While God is saving you for marriage, learn how to be a servant unto Him first. Marriage requires you to serve your partner and cater to their needs and wants. If you don't know how to be a servant unto God first, then how can you serve someone in a marriage? Being a servant unto God will teach you how to weigh out the needs of the Father. This will allow God to put you in a position where you are giving all of your time to serving Him and pleasing Him.

Once you do that, this will show God that He has your attention. After a while, God will become your main focus. Once you begin to feel like God is all that you need, that's when He will send someone to you.

"When your focus is not on God, then your spouse will never come at the time that you may desire. But the moment that all of your focus goes toward serving and pleasing God, then they will come."
– Kianna Brooks

Therefore, when you are being a servant unto Jesus Christ, continue to commit yourself unto Him and eventually He will lead you to your spouse. Job 23:11 says, "My foot hath held his steps, his way have I kept, and not declined."

- Have a Teachable Spirit

Marriage is a lifetime commitment that requires you to commit yourself to your partner for a lifetime. You have to make sure you are in a position mentally, physically, emotionally, and spiritually to be able to be committed to a person through marriage. So, how can we become ready for marriage? When you begin to read the Word of God, He will teach you how to carry yourself until your spouse comes. Matthew 6:33 says, "But seek ye first the kingdom of God, and his righteousness; and all these things shall be added unto you."

When you are waiting to become a spouse, ask God to give you a humble, teachable spirit. Allow Him to give you the material that you need to help prepare you for marriage. This will be a preparation stage that you will have to go through while you are waiting. God will use this time to teach you godly wisdom, how to have compassion for others, and how to grow into the man or woman that He has called you to be.

If you want to see yourself progressing in these things, then you have to be willing to learn from God. Also, make sure that you have an ear to hear from God so that you can become more comfortable in knowing God's voice.

"You can't listen to God's directions for your life clearly if you have other voices leading you in other directions."
– Kianna Brooks

- Be Prepared

One way to prepare yourself for marriage is by understanding your self-value. Why? Because some people are so desperate to be in a relationship with someone, they begin to date less than what they are worth. There's an old saying: "There's somebody out there for everybody." If you wait on God's perfect timing, then you will see that there is somebody out there waiting for you. Also, don't waste time with people who will not pursue you in marriage. Instead, strive for purity, don't commit fornication, be faithful unto God, and He will teach you how to be faithful unto Him.

Lastly, I've learned that we have to use this time wisely while we are waiting for our spouses to come. As you wait for them, learn how to cook, clean, manage your money, and start saving up for your wedding day. These things will help you become successful in your relationship and your marriage. This last section will teach you how to do these things while you wait for your spouse.

Women, God will not send you husbands for the purpose of:

- Getting married for the title ("wife")
- Because you're tired of being lonely
- Using him for what he can bring to the table
- Keeping him for what he has to offer
- Desiring to move in with him

- Expecting him to pay for all of your bills
- Using him because he's weak-minded
- Because he's weak-minded, you will marry him so that you can play the dominant role in the marriage
- Using him just to have an extra hand around the house and to help take some of the load off of you
- Using him to help you take care of your kids
- Marrying him because you know that he can afford your dream wedding
- Marrying him because he has riches and wealth
- Marrying him because his family is financially stable
- Using him to gain access from his family
- Using him for money
- Counting his pockets
- Desiring his body lustfully
- Marrying him to fulfill all of your sexual desires in the bedroom

Men, God will not send you a wife for the purpose of:

- Marrying her because you're tired of being single
- Using her because you need a place to stay
- Borrowing her car for your personal use
- Using her just to have someone to cook and

clean for you

- Using her for what she has to offer

- Using her because of what she can bring to the table

- Marrying her because she already has her life together

- Taking advantage of her being financially stable

- Using her for money

- Gaining access to things she has that can be beneficial to you

- Accessing her parents' wealth

- Using her to help you take care of your kids

- Using her because she's weak minded

- Marrying her so that you can control her every move

- Expecting her to be the provider within the marriage because you're too lazy to get a job

- Marrying her for bragging rights

- Marrying her because she has a nice body and desiring her body sexually

- Marrying her because she is beautiful and idolizing her face based off of what the world thinks you should have as a wife

Tips: Preparing Yourself for Marriage

Clean Up Your Mess

Start cleaning up after yourself! Don't expect God to send you a spouse so they can keep the house tidied up for you. I heard a wise man once say, "If you are going to be nasty before the wedding, then you will be nasty in the marriage. Marrying a person doesn't change them; it just changes their last name!" Only God can touch someone's heart for it to bring forth a change. It will be very stressful to keep up with a person who is nasty and unorganized. Because once you clean up something, they will mess it right back up, and then you will only find yourself getting frustrated with the person. That's why it's best to work on this problem before marriage. Always remember that cleanliness is a form of godliness. Ezekiel 36:25-27 (ESV) says, "I will sprinkle clean water on you, and you shall be clean from all your uncleannesses, and from all your idols I will cleanse you. And I will give you a new heart, and a new spirit I will put within you. And I will remove the heart of stone from your flesh and give you a heart of flesh. And I will put my Spirit within you, and cause you to walk in my statutes and be careful to obey my rules."

Cook for Yourself

Practice cooking meals that you see on TV, social media, Google, or YouTube. If you don't know how to cook, then ask somebody to teach you how to prepare a home-cooked meal. Other ways of learning how to cook can be accessed right through our phones. Google "How to prepare a home-cooked meal for beginners". Lastly, pray and ask the Holy Spirit to show you how to cook. Always remember that the Holy Spirit is here to teach you. He is the world's greatest chef, and He would love to show you how to cook if you ask Him and let Him. Revelation 3:20 (ESV) says, "Behold, I stand at the door and knock. If anyone hears my voice and opens the door, I will come in to him and eat with him, and he with me."

Start Saving Up Money for Your Wedding Day

It's best to start early! Make a sacrifice by putting up a specific amount for your wedding day. This will help mitigate the cost of the wedding. Since you don't know the specific date of your wedding, use this idea to help you save up some extra cash. Matthew 25:27 (ESV) says, "Then you ought to have invested my money with the bankers, and at my coming I should have received what was my own with interest."

Manage Your Money

- 1 Corinthians 16:2 (AMP) says, "On the first day of every week each one of you is to put something aside, in proportion to his prosperity, and save it so that no collections [will need to] be made when I come."

- Ask God to teach you how to manage your money.

- Pray over your money that it will grow and be prosperous in your life.

- Always set aside money for your tithes and offering.

- Observe the amount of money that you spend within a month's timing.

- When your mail comes in, add up every bill that you are obligated to pay within a month. See if it is a necessity or a want. If it's a necessity, then you need to have it. If it's a want, then get rid of it and save your money.

- Make a savings account. Save for a specific cause.

- Continue to save up for your wedding day.

- Don't get a joint banking account with your partner if you are not married to them. Your banking account should only be shared with your spouse.

- Put yourself on a budget and minimize the times that you go out to eat within a week.

- Stop being a shopaholic. Go shopping every

once in a while.

- Building up your credit score is a form of managing your money.
- Start investing in your future. You have to set up the life that you want to have. Invest in things that will be huge assets to your life. Also, don't expect anyone to do anything for you that you can already do for yourself.

Date: ____________________

NOTES

____
____
____
____
____
____
____
____
____
____
____
____
____
____
____
____
____
____
____
____
____

"'For I know the plans I have for you,' declares the Lord, 'plans to prosper you and not to harm you, plans to give you hope and a future.'" Jeremiah 29:11 (NIV)

Chapter 11

†

The Gift That Comes From Waiting

"Live joyfully with the wife whom thou lovest all the days of the life of thy vanity, which he hath given thee under the sun, all the days of thy vanity: for that is thy portion in this life, and in thy labour which thou takest under the sun."
Ecclesiastes 9:9

James 1:17 says, "Every good gift and every perfect gift is from above, and cometh down from the Father of lights, with whom is no variableness, neither shadow of turning."

The Gift That Comes from Waiting

We all know that every good and perfect gift comes from above (James 1:17). When it comes to finding true love, we have to wait on God to send us our precious gifts, which is our spouses. Once that person gets here, that will be the blessing that we will receive from waiting. Earlier in the book, we discussed how Rachel was Jacob's perfect gift that came from waiting. Well, the key to finding a spouse with great qualities such as Jacob's requires you to wait for them, have patience, believe, and receive them once they come. When God begins to send people in your life, ask Him, "Is this the spouse that You desire for me to have?" If Jacob was able to marry the person he desired, then why can't we? As Christians, we need to know that God allows us to court while waiting for our spouses. During this time, we are getting to know the people before marriage. After courting your partner, you begin to think that you have found the person of your dreams. When you begin to realize that God has sent you your spouse, don't be in a rush to get married. Take time out to get to know your partner so you can learn more about them and their character. Once you learn the character of your partner, then you can make the decision to marry them or not. If you see that this person has a possibility of being in your future, then ask God if you should marry them. Once He tells you what to do, then you will know what to do next that will be beneficial for you and your future spouse. The goal for this chapter is to teach Christian singles how to start new journeys with the ones that they may love. It will teach them how to marry the spouses that God has for them, how to transition from being single to married, how to receive godly counsel in their marriages, and how to commit themselves to their partners for a lifetime. I pray that this last chapter will give you hope in finding the spouse that God has for you!

Marrying The Person that God Has for You

Proverbs 5:18 says, "Let thy fountain be blessed: and rejoice with the wife of thy youth." After learning your partner, you begin to realize that you're willing to take your relationship to the next level! Before proposing to them, pray and ask God is this the spouse that He has for you. Once you feel that God has answered your prayers, begin to intercede on their behalf and yours. I read an article that said, "One of the keys to finding the right marriage partner is understanding the difference between lust and love."

"Lust" is the act of desiring someone for sex and what their body has to offer. "Love" is the quality of character, not emotional attachment. Learn the kind of love that we learned through Jesus Christ.

The Bible says in John 3:16, "For God so loved the world, that he gave his only begotten Son, that whosoever believeth in him shall not perish, but have everlasting life." Remember, no matter how much you may love or care for a person, your relationship should always draw you closer to God.

Lastly, if you feel like you're not ready for marriage, then don't let anyone pressure you into getting married. Matthew 19:11-12 (MSG) says, "But Jesus said, 'Not everyone is mature enough to live a married life. It requires a certain aptitude and grace. Marriage isn't for everyone. Some, from birth seemingly, never give marriage a thought. Others never get asked – or accepted. And some decide not to get married for kingdom reasons. But if you're capable of growing into the largeness of marriage, do it.'"

Transitioning from Being Single to Married

"Some people are not worthy enough to inherit your future. So you have to be cautious about who you allow in your life. Once you find that special someone, cherish that moment with them forever because you are worth every second of it."
– Kianna Brooks

Now, as you wait to receive your special gift from God (your spouse), He will allow you to come into holy matrimony with the man or woman of your dreams. The moment that you say "I do", you and your partner become joined together as one flesh! Ephesians 5:31 says, "For this cause shall a man leave his father and mother, and shall be joined unto his wife, and they two shall be one flesh." Now that you are married, you and your spouse have to learn how to transition from being single to married. When you are transitioning, you are making a lifestyle change that will be for the better for you and your spouse. If you don't know how to adapt to this transition, then it's going to be difficult for you to survive in your marriage. For those of you who are single, this next section will teach you how to transition into a marriage once you get married.

Yes, adapting from a single life to a married life can be hard at first, but the way that you carried yourself when you were single will not work once you get married. Fifty percent of marriages don't work because people go in with the wrong mindset. A lot of couples don't want to get rid of most of their old ways once they get married. If you want your marriage to work, then you will have to learn how to sacrifice some things for your partner. Jacob (in the Bible) may not have wanted to work an additional seven years to be able to marry Rachel, but because of the love that he had for her, he was willing to give up his time laboring to be able to receive her hand in marriage. The following are some great tips about things that you may have to adapt to once you get married.

Things You Have to Adapt to Once You Get Married

- Honoring your spouse's parents
- Dealing with the loss of a loved one
- Sharing thoughts freely
- Discussing sensitive topics
- Accepting your partner's religion
- Building a God-based foundation
- Money/financial needs
- Being the only source of income
- Enjoying spending time with your spouse
- Date nights/restaurants/entertainment
- Vacations and travel
- Giving them compliments
- Reminding them of the love you share
- Establishing a home with your spouse
- Helping out around the house/doing outside chores
- Having intimacy
- Pregnancy
- Clothing and feeding the children
- The proper education for your children
- Supporting each other's dreams
- Being okay with your spouse quitting their full-time job to go back to school or being okay

with your spouse if they decide to quit their full-time job to follow their dreams

Receive Spiritual Guidance for Your Marriage

Psalm 32:8 (ESV) says, "I will instruct you and teach you in the way you should go; I will counsel you with my eye upon you." Once a month, my pastor holds a counseling session at our church called "Marriage Workshop". Marriage Workshop gives couples spiritual guidance in their relationships or marriages. She believes that every relationship needs spiritual maintenance and if you want God to be in the midst of your relationship, then you need to have marriage counseling.

If you are in a relationship or marriage that is ordained by God, then you need to have spiritual counseling to help make the relationship work. Spiritual maintenance is receiving godly counseling from your spiritual leader, mentor, or advisor. These people are here to help you and your spouse's relationship grow stronger in Christ. Going to see a marriage counselor doesn't mean that you have problems in your marriage; it just means you want to receive spiritual guidance to help your relationship. Going to marriage counseling will show you and your partner which areas you may desire to work on. Wanting to excel in your marriage with your partner shows them that you want to grow together as a couple.

This will give you guys quality time to spend with each other while helping one another grow spiritually. When you begin to receive sound doctrine from your spiritual leader, never take their time for granted. Your pastor spiritually sits at the feet of Jesus to receive spiritual guidance to help you. This wisdom and knowledge will feed into your spirit so that you can grow spiritually. Also, this knowledge will teach you how to stay submissive unto God, His word, and your future spouse. John 16:13 says, "Howbeit when he, the Spirit of truth, is come, he will guide you into all truth: for he shall not speak of himself; but whatsoever he shall hear, that shall he speak: and he will shew you things to come." This last section will teach you how to become submissive to your partner. It will show you how to be committed to your spouse once you become married.

Commit Yourself to Your Partner for a Lifetime

Ephesians 5:22-24 says, "Wives, submit yourselves unto your own husbands, as unto the Lord. For the husband is the head of the wife, even as Christ is the head of the church: and he is the saviour of the body. Therefore as the church is subject unto Christ, so let the wives be to their own husbands in every thing." Once you become married, you have to understand that you are no longer classified as "single". After realizing that, learn how to include God and your spouse in everything that you do. This shows them that you're trying to stay committed to them and your marriage. Committing yourself in a marriage is learning how to get rid of the term "I" and focusing more on the term "us". The day that you take your vows, ask God to teach you how to submit and commit yourself unto Him and your spouse. These transitions will require you to commit yourself to your partner for a lifetime.

Next, another form of committing yourself is being submissive. Being submissive to your partner is submitting yourself to their wants, needs, and desires. It's teaching you how to become faithful to them and the marriage. If you don't know how to be faithful to you partner, ask God to show you how to submit yourself to them. 1 Peter 3:5-7 (ESV) says, "For this is how the holy women who hoped in God used to adorn themselves, by submitting to their own husbands, as Sarah obeyed Abraham, calling him lord. And you are her children, if you do good and do not fear anything that is frightening. Likewise, husbands, live with your wives in an understanding way, showing honor to the woman as the weaker vessel, since they are heirs with you of the grace of life, so that your prayers may not be hindered."

Also, when it comes to getting married to the right one, God's main focus is that you know that it is not a spouse you cannot live without but rather Him (God) you cannot live without. When you realize that you cannot live without God, then you will know that only having a spouse will not be enough to live with. Sharing your life with them and God will be all that you need. Being married is not an easy journey, but spending a lifetime with the person you may love is worth every second of it. Once you get married, stay committed to your spouse and share love with your partner so that you can grow together as one. From that day forth, you will be dedicating your life to the spouse God has given to you.

Developing a Healthy Marriage

- Commit yourself unto God, your spouse, and your children.
- Learn how to be submissive to them.
- Make it your duty to remain faithful unto God and your spouse.
- Love them just like Christ loves the church.
- Build a prayer life with your partner.
- Learn them.
- Set aside time for the relationship.
- Set goals for your marriage.
- Stay on task meeting your spouse's personal needs.
- Keep your marriage founded on the Word of God. Studying God's Word together will help you

gain a personal relationship with them and the Holy Spirit.

- Fight for your marriage through prayer and know that God will keep you.
- No matter what the circumstances are, you will have to continue to make things work because God will be greater than the circumstances that you may face.
- Even if you and your spouse don't get to accomplish everything that you may desire in life, still cherish the moments that you are able to share together as a couple.
- Once you get married, use the Word of God as a weapon towards the enemy when he tries to come against your marriage.
- Once you get married, grow with your spouse spiritually, mentally, emotionally, and through intimacy.
- Men, be the providers in your marriage. Women, be the nurturers.

CLOSING

Well, this is it! You finally have all the material you need in finding your new Mr. or Mrs. Right. One day, my Mr. Right will find me, and he will become the precious gift that I have been waiting for. Hopefully, your true love is out there waiting for your arrival as well. While we were studying the Word of God, Jacob and Rachel's story taught us how to wait on God for our spouses. Ruth and Boaz's story teaches us how to continue to serve God until they come.

So, men, be like Jacob and wait for your Rachel. Women, be like Ruth and wait for God to send you your Boaz. As you wait for them, look to the hills from which cometh your help and know that God will keep His promises to you. Continue to pray and ask God to help guide you while you wait to get married. Stay focused by putting your trust in God and knowing that one day He will send you your spouse. Matthew 19:4-6 says, "And he answered and said unto them, Have ye not read, that he which made them at the beginning made them male and female, And said, For this cause shall a man leave father and mother, and shall cleave to his wife: and they twain shall be one flesh? Wherefore they are no more twain, but one flesh. What therefore God hath joined together, let not man put asunder."

Dear future husband, I'm waiting.........

Closing Prayer: Waiting for True Love

Ephesians 5:25 says, "Husbands, love your wives, even as Christ also loved the church, and gave himself for it..."

Our Father,

I come to you in the name of Jesus asking for guidance as I wait for my future spouse. As I continue to wait, give me patience to stay steadfast in Your Word. Teach me truth so that I can grow in Your Word spiritually. While I'm waiting, show me who my God-given spouse is and send me the person who You desire for me to have. Make me the spouse that you desire for me to become. And let my heart be pure to the one that you have placed in my life to marry.

1 John 3:2-3 (NIV) says, "Dear friends, now we are children of God, and what we will be has not yet been made known. But we know that when Christ appears, we shall be like him, for we shall see him as he is. All who have this hope in him purify themselves, just as he is pure."

Lord, before I give my heart to my spouse, become my first love so that I can share it with You. That way, when my spouse comes, I can know how to share it with them. Never let me love my spouse more than I love You, but teach me how to love them unconditionally. 1 Corinthians 13:4-8 (AMP) says, "Love endures with patience and serenity, love is kind and thoughtful, and is not jealous or envious; love does not brag and is not proud or arrogant. It is not rude; it is not self-seeking, it is not provoked [nor overly sensitive and easily angered]; it does not take into account a wrong endured. It does not rejoice at injustice, but rejoices with the truth [when right and truth prevail]. Love bears all things [regardless of what comes], believes all things [looking for the best in each one], hopes all things [remaining steadfast during difficult times], endures all things [without weakening]. Love never fails [it never fades nor ends]..." Dear God, from this day forth, I commit myself to You and my future spouse.

In Jesus' name I pray. Amen!

Dear future spouse,

____
____
____
____
____
____
____
____
____
____
____
____
____
____
____
____
____
____
____
____
____
____
____
____
____
____
____

SIGNATURE: ________________________________

DATE: __________________

Your Wedding Day

Hurry, hurry! Your wedding day is near. Today, I hear wedding bells! I see groomsmen putting on their tuxedos and bridesmaids putting on their gowns. On this day, God will be joining two people who love each other together in holy matrimony. Through this wedding ceremony, I see God tying together three cords that cannot be broken or cut. Ecclesiastes 4:12 says, "And if one prevail against him, two shall withstand him; and a threefold cord is not quickly broken." The first cord symbolizes the man because he is the head over his wife and their household. It's his job to take care of his wife by being the provider to her and their family. The second cord symbolizes the woman. It's her job to bear her husband's children and become the nurturer in the marriage. She's more of the caregiver. The third cord represents God. It is His duty to protect the marriage and make sure that no one comes against it. With these three cords being in covenant together, nothing will be able to come between them. If someone or something tries to come against this marriage, then they will fall and not stand. Therefore, get married to someone that's going to be in covenant with you and God. On your wedding day, make sure you make it your duty to love them just like Christ loved the church. Ephesians 5:25-26 says, "Husbands, love your wives, even as Christ also loved the church, and gave himself for it; That he might sanctify and cleanse it with the washing of water by the word..." Until this day approaches, follow behind God. Allow him to be the demonstrator and show you what to wait for. John 12:26 says, " If any man serve me, let him follow me; and where I am, there shall also my servant be: if any man serve me, him will my Father honour."

Marriage Date: ________ /________ /________

A NOTE FROM THE AUTHOR

Life is a beautiful journey, so why not spend it with the one that you may love? 1 Corinthians 13:4 (AMP) says, "Love endures with patience and serenity, love is kind and thoughtful, and is not jealous or envious; love does not brag and is not proud or arrogant." While studying, I learned that the word "love" needs to become an action and not just a feeling. That's why I believe the saying, "True love awaits those who wait on God." This book is to teach Christian singles how to start new journeys with the ones that they may love. It will teach them how to wait on God for their soulmates, how to transition from being single to married, how to marry the spouses that God has for them, and how to commit themselves to their partners for a lifetime. Hopefully, one day God will be joining two people who love each other together in holy matrimony. I pray that this book will give you hope in finding the spouse that God has for you!

"A fairytale only has a happy ending when the queen waits for her king to arrive. Trust the process; it's worth the wait."
– Kianna Brooks

REFERENCES

1. https://quotespics.net/love-couple-drawings-pics-quotes-and-images-2016/
2. https://www.powerofpositivity.com/relationship-walls
3. https://www.genuinesuccess.co.uk/a-winding-path-to-success/
4. https://www.shutterstock.com/video/clip-14518783-rainbow-flag-commonly-gay-pride-lgbt-waving
5. http://jesuscircle.me/does-god-have-a-statement-on-homosexuality/
6. https://redro.pl/fototapeta-mlody-mezczyzna-czyta-ksiazke,6172817
7. http://www.fabulousfoilprints.com/cat-pages.html/MM_8x10_pics.html
8. https://activechristianity.org/what-is-the-spirit-of-pentecost
9. https://www.themindfulword.org/2012/community-matthew-fox-end-loneliness/
10. http://clipart-library.com/choir-singers-cliparts.html
11. https://thoughtcatalog.com/farah-ayaad/2017/05/this-is-what-letting-go-really-means-because-its-more-than-moving-on/
12. https://www.thegospelcoalition.org/article/four-things-god-says-singles/
13. http://www.umc.org/what-we-believe/what-does-it-mean-to-be-saved-to-accept-jesus-as-your-personal-savior33.
14. https://theideators.co/why-being-single-in-your-early-20s-is-awesome/
15. https://www.merrchant.com/blog/what-is-true-love-signs-and-characteristics-of-true-love/
16. https://www.ukrainegiftdelivery.com/Heart-Shaped-Roses-Arrangement-p/105.htm
17. https://www.britannica.com/topic/same-sex-marriage/biography/Rachel-biblical-figure

ABOUT THE AUTHOR

Kianna Brooks is a native of Shreveport, Louisiana. She has been a born-again Christian since 1994. She was led to Christ through her parents, Mitchell and Joy Brooks. By the leading of the Holy Spirit and watching her Christian parents' love story, Kianna was inspired to write Single and Saved Waiting for Mr. Right. Writing this book has now made Kianna the author of her first Christian book. She believes that true love awaits those who wait on God. She says this is just the beginning of writing many more Christian novels that will be published in the future. Her favorite scripture is Philippians 4:13– "I can do all things through Christ which strengthens me." (KJV) Studying this scripture has helped Kianna accomplish many goals in life that have set her up for success. She feels that without God or using this scripture to motivate her, her life would mean nothing. Kianna has accomplished a lot of things in life for only being in her twenties. Kianna has an associate degree from Southern University at Shreveport and is now working on her bachelor's degree in business administration. Kianna is also a motivational speaker. She loves speaking life into many of the youths and young adults in her city. Many colleges, schools, and churches have invited Kianna to speak to and help inspire their youths and young adults. She believes that working with youths helps them form a deeper relationship with God and helps them discover the plans that He has for their lives. Kianna is so grateful for these opportunities because she knows that it was nobody but God who placed her there. To this day, she is still striving to become the woman who God has called her to be. She believes that God has truly called her to do great things for Him in this season! Kianna's motto is: "Live your life to the fullest, love unconditionally, and inspire everyone that crosses your path. Bigger, better, greater!"

J. Kenkade
PUBLISHING®

Also Available from J. Kenkade Publishing

ISBN: 978-1-944486-25-9
Visit www.drniokasmith.com
Author: Dr. Nioka Smith

Sexually abused by her father at the age of 14, pregnant at the age of 17, and a nervous breakdown at the age of 28, Dr. Nioka Smith's painful past almost killed her, until the voice of the Lord guided her into destroying strongholds and reversing Satan's plan for her life. DIVAS Unchained is the powerful chain-breaking reality of the many unfortunate strongholds our women and girls face. Dr. Nioka uses her divine gift to help women and girls break free from destructive life cycles and prosper in all areas of life. Satan has lied to you. It's time to expose his lies. It's time to break free!

Also Available from J. Kenkade Publishing

ISBN: 978-1-955186-02-5
Visit www.amazon.com
Author: Indigo Manning

In this life, there are certain burdens a godly woman will inevitably face. Indigo Manning has seen firsthand how real those burdens can be, but her testimony is that there is joy to be found in serving our Creator because He does not intend for us to shoulder those burdens on our own. When we cast our cares upon Him and ground ourselves in the purpose He has instilled in all of us, we are able to flourish as mothers, wives, sisters, and friends. Perhaps more important than all of those relationships, however, is a woman's relationship with herself. Though trials may come, if we all do the work of self-reflection and personal stewardship, we can maintain identities rooted in Christ and allow the Holy Spirit to work through us.

Also Available from
J. Kenkade Publishing

ISBN: 978-1-955186-03-2
Visit www.amazon.com
Author: Janice Buckley

Scripture does not say "yesterday's" faith or "tomorrow's" faith. It simply says "now" faith. Right now, immediately! With faith the size of a mustard seed, you can move mountains. God has given us the same power and authority to speak and see the manifestation thereof. What better time than now to start doing what God has called you to do? What are you waiting for? I must warn you: the purpose of this book is not to tell you what your Purpose is, but I want to encourage you to find your Purpose by seeking God, who is able to do exceedingly and abundantly above all that we can ask or think.

Also Available from J. Kenkade Publishing

ISBN: 978-1-944486-90-7
Visit www.amazon.com
Author: Thomas Gray

Marriage by the Book is a profound and practical guidebook designed to help you cultivate a deeper relationship based on sound Biblical wisdom. Written by Pastor Thomas Gray, this book combines proven step-by-step strategies of practical relationships with spiritual lessons and Bible-based principles to help you overcome conflicts, improve your communication, handle difficult discussions, and celebrate the unique union and covenant which unites you together with God. Marriage by the Book is ideal for both new and seasoned couples who are searching for better ways to strengthen their relationship and fulfill their promises to God.

Pastor Thomas Gray: P.O. Box 360041/Dallas, TX 75336
www.twdcdaltx.org (972) 926-3762

www.ingramcontent.com/pod-product-compliance
Lightning Source LLC
LaVergne TN
LVHW010058110826
845155LV00028B/398